Presented to:

Amanda Proctor

Presented by:

Sis Myrna Rose

On this date:

December 22, 1996

Merry Christmas

An Awesome Bible Rhyme Time
© MCMXCVI by Phil A. Smouse

ISBN 1-55748-886-X

I Love Ruthie
© MCMXCV by Phil A. Smouse

Why, Oh Why? Oh Me, Oh My!
© MCMXCV by Phil A. Smouse

A Jonah Day
© MCMXCIV by Phil A. Smouse

Pete, Feet, and Fish to Eat
© MCMXCIV by Phil A. Smouse

All rights reserved. No part of this publication may be reproduced or transmitted in any form or by any means without written permission of the publisher.

Published by Barbour & Company, Inc.
      P.O. Box 719
      Uhrichsville, Ohio 44683
      e-mail: books<barbour@tusco.net>

Member of the
Evangelical Christian
Publishers Association

Printed in the United States of America

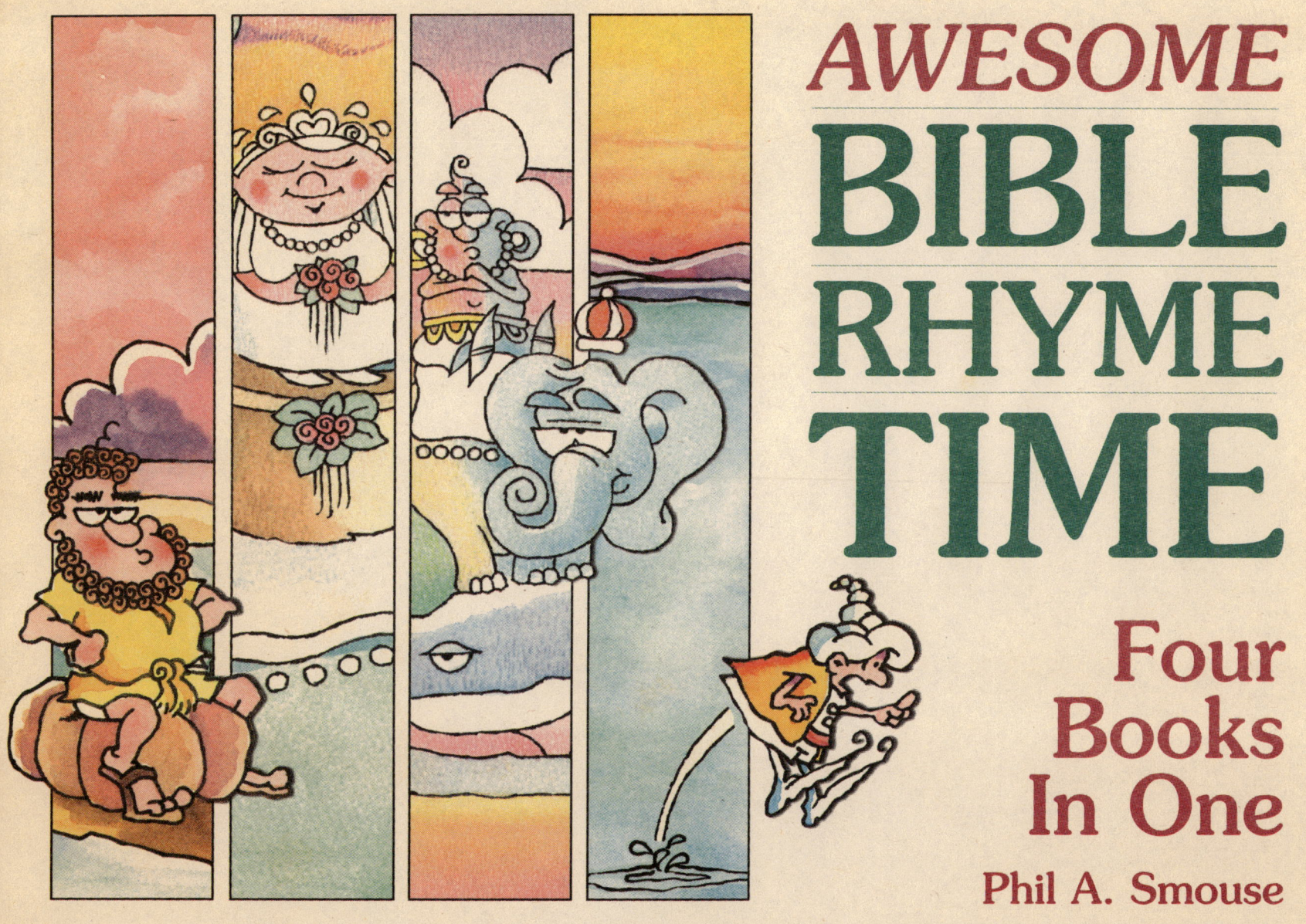

For Annette, Danielle, and David
who are so very precious in His sight.

Note to Parents

It was a dark and stormy night...

almost seven years ago when my daughter and I went to the library for the very first time. We picked up a copy of *Green Eggs and Ham* by Dr. Seuss.

To my utter amazement, I remembered almost *every word* in the book, even though it had been close to twenty-five years since I last cracked the cover.

And then it happened...

"What if it was My Word you remembered so well?" said God's still, small voice. I never considered writing and illustrating for children before that moment. My sights were set on the newspaper comics pages. God had quite a different plan, however. A much better plan! You're holding it in your hands right now.

In these very confusing times what could be more important for our children than a solid understanding of God's Word? Like the men and women whose job it is to spot counterfeit currency, our kids need to know *the real thing* so well, they can recognize the slightest error immediately. My purpose in "translating" these Bible stories is to develop that excitement and desire for God's Word in the hearts of your children (and provide them, and *you,* with a wee bit of fun in the process!).

continued...

*"The grass withers and the flowers fall,
but the word of our God stands forever...*

*The Sovereign Lord comes with power...
He tends his flock like a shepherd:
He gathers the lambs in his arms and carries them close to his heart."*

Isaiah 40:8-11 NIV

As you read through these stories with your precious little ones, I hope they bring back some special memories for you as well. I'm praying that every "little lamb" who reads this book will some day find what I've found: Jesus Christ, the true Son of the living God, will forgive anything—*anything*—tear up the ticket and declare us "not guilty"... *Perfect in His Sight.*

God made you just right. You are so very special to Him.
He loves you *just the way you are.*

Enjoy!

Phil A. Smouse

I LOVE RUTHIE

The Story of Ruth

BY PHIL A. SMOUSE

A Barbour Book

"It can't be true! I can't go on!
Oh, everything we had is gone!"
Naomi wept. Poor Ruthie cried.

Naomi's precious sons had died!

And oh, one precious, priceless son,
Naomi's son, that very one,
was Ruthie's *husband!* Lord above!
Her one-and-only one true love!

Now, sometimes when it rains it pours, and this time it would pour for sure!

For evil people ruled the land
as evil people sometimes can
and sometimes will and sometimes do,
when you and I allow them to!

From here to there, from there to here,
the food began to disappear!
It filled the people full of fear—
yes, full of fear from ear to ear!

"Orpah! Ruth!" Naomi cried.
"The time has come. We must decide.
We have to leave. We cannot stay.
We cannot stay, not now, no way!

From north to south, from west to east,
the men are gone. Extinct. Deceased!
Without a man," Naomi said,
"WE'RE ALL ABOUT AS GOOD AS DEAD!"

(Now be cool, some things were different then,
so don't get too upset, amen?)

"Just look at me! I'm old and wrinkled,
sagged and bagged and crook'd and crinkled,
crumpled, puckered, nooked and crannied,
Rip-Van-Winkled, grayed and grannied!

Oh, there's just no hope in sight
to find another Mister Right,
or even just a Daffy Duck,
an Elmer Fudd, or Mister Yuck!

The time has come! The time is now.
The time has come right now and how!
You must return, you *must*, I say,
return back home, right now, today!"

Naomi prayed that they would bite
and Orpah knew that she was right.
She packed her bags without a fight
and left for home that very night.

But oh, not Ruth.
Not her. No way!
She had a thing
or two to say....

"I can't return. I want to stay.
I will NOT go 'right now, today!'"

"For where you are is where I'll be.
And when you stay, you'll stay with me.
And when you die, I'll die with you.
And THAT is what I'm going to do!

Your God will be MY God and He
will surely care for you and me!"

Oh, what a thing for Ruth to say.
That kind of thing can make your day,
and make you shout *"hip-hip hooray!"*

They hugged and kissed, then packed up tight
and left for Bethlehem that night.

"Naomi! Is it really true?
What happened, girl? Just look at you!

Your hair! Your clothes! Your shoes! Your toes!
Your eyes, your ears, your mouth, your nose!
You're looking pale. You're looking thin.
In fact, if we may say again,
you're really looking more akin
to something that the cat dragged in!"

(Well, things looked bad, the way things can,
but listen now, God had a plan....)

"Oh Naomi, please don't cry.
Oh please don't cry. I'll tell you why!

I'll find a farm. I'll be real nice.
I'll ask them once or maybe twice
to take our jugs and jars and sacks
and fill them full of treats and snacks.

Yes, crumbs and morsels, flakes and flecks,
leftover kernels, crumbs and specks.
A black banana! Bagels! Lox!
Some cheese stuck to a pizza box!

I'll beg and plead. I'll sob and bleat!
I'll ask them for a tasty treat—
An itsy-bitsy, teeny-weeny,
tiny scrap for us to eat!"

25

So off she went. She did her thing.
She did it never noticing
that someone had been fastening
his bulging eyes on everything!

"Who *IS* that girl out in my field
and what's she doing?" Boaz squealed.
"Look *AT* that hair. Look *AT* those eyes!
Excuse me just one minute, guys,
I've got to go and socialize!"

(No, Boaz wasn't one to miss
an opportunity like this!)

He shaved his toes. He licked his lips.
He checked his teeth for cracks and chips.
He combed the bugs out of his hair,
yes, Don Juan double-debonair
with savoir-faire extraordinaire!

(Now, don't be quick to judge, amen?
Well, don't think what you're thinking then!
For *Boaz* was a gentleman.)

"Please stay with us. Take what you need.
Take what you need and more, indeed!"

He loaded up all Ruthie's sacks
and jugs and jars with treats and snacks.
Yes, *it WAS* true love at first sight—
a double thumping-heart delight!

She headed home. Oh, what she'd found!
Her world was turning upside-down.
She ran the whole way back to town
about ten feet above the ground.

"I'm telling you, tonight's the night,"
Naomi grinned, "and if I'm right,
there's only one thing left to do
to get that man to say *I DO!*"

(So do they did. Oh, *DID* they do....)

They fluffed and puffed. They crimped and curled.
They powdered, sweet-perfumed, and pearled!
They thanked the Lord. They sang His praise!
They marveled at His wondrous ways!

And off she went into the night
to have and hold her Mister Right—
her Mister Shining-Armored Knight—
her straight from heaven-sent delight!

34

Now, as I'm sure that you supposed
Boaz said "YES!" when Ruth proposed!
Yes, *RUTH* proposed. That's what I said.
Just look it up, go right ahead.

They tied the knot and lived to be
quite happy ever-afterly.
And soon God blessed them with a son,
a precious, little baby one!

But wait! This story's far from done.
Because their son, he was the one
who had a son, who had a kid
known as King David. Yes, he did!

And David was the Great, Great, Great,
Great, Great (times three, times one, plus eight)
Great Grand-dad of a man whose wife
you've probably heard of all your life.

A man whose son, to be precise,
was Jesus. *No?!* YES! *Jesus Christ!*

Just take a second, think it through.
Oh, what God will go and do!

For God is love and love is kind,
the kindest that you'll ever find,
the kindest that you'll ever see,
that's something else, don't you agree!?

WHY, OH WHY? OH ME, OH MY!
The Story of Job

BY PHIL A. SMOUSE

A Barbour Book

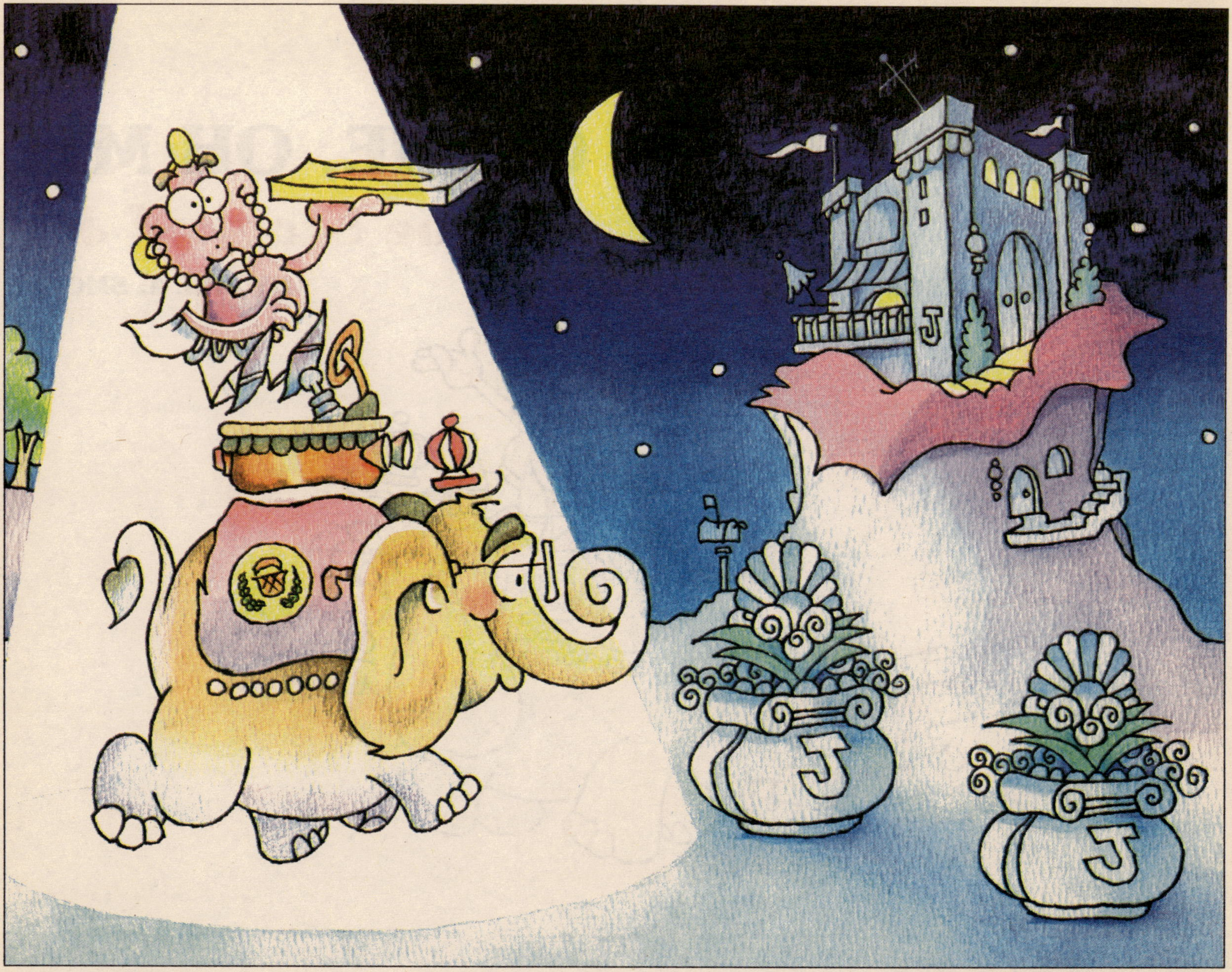
J
J
J

"Have you noticed my servant? He's gentle and kind
and our hearts are so sweetly, completely entwined.
He's as good as it gets. Yes, the cream of the crop.
The pick of the litter. The tip of the top!"

"And why not?" croaked the devil. "He's as rich as a king.
Why, you've never withheld even one little thing.
Take away all those whistles and hooters and bells
and I'll bet it's a whole different story he tells!"

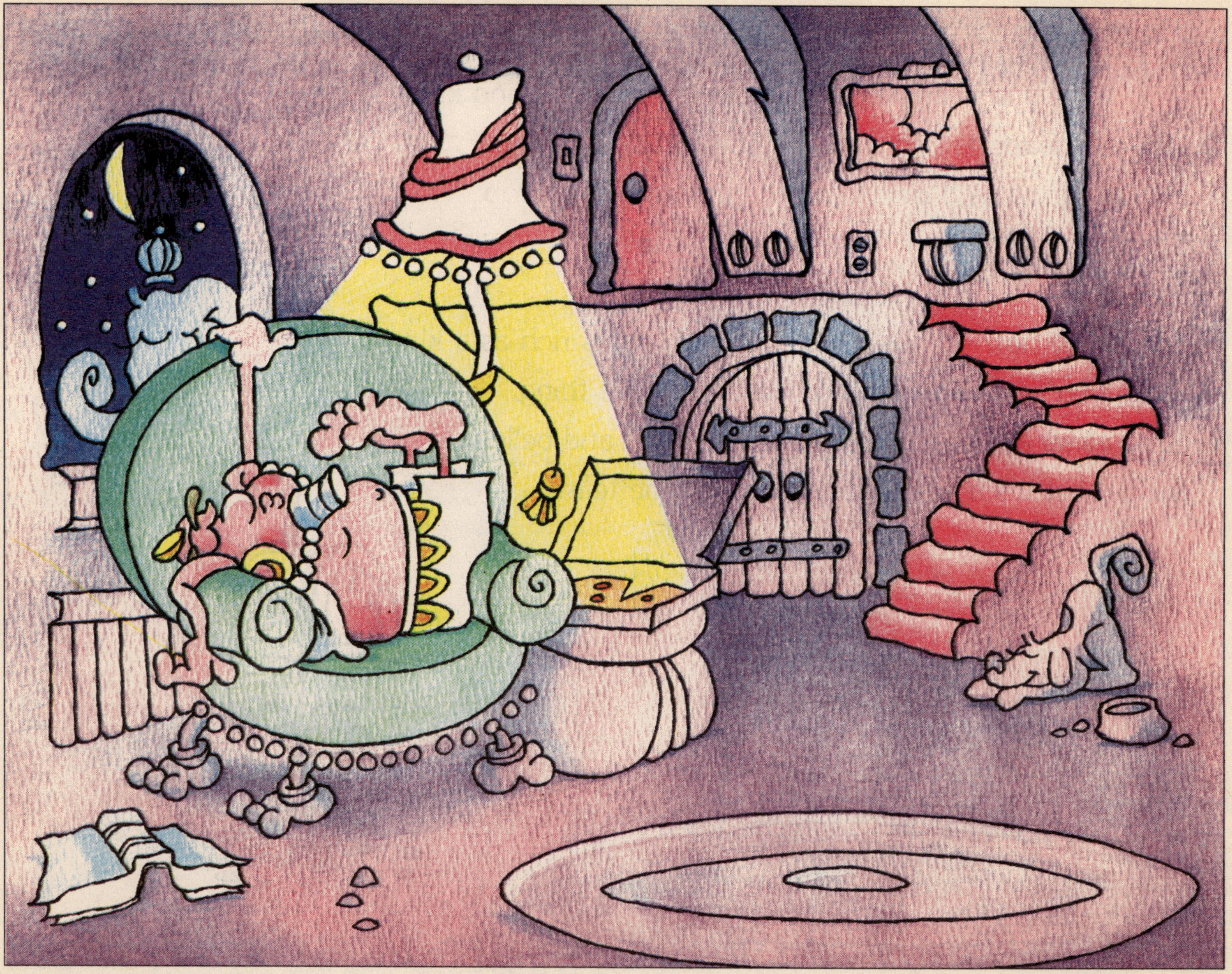

Well, that night while Job snoozed in his big easy chair,
as he snurgled and snorgled, he got quite a scare.
Three men came abusting right into the room
and proceeded to fill him with gloom and with doom!

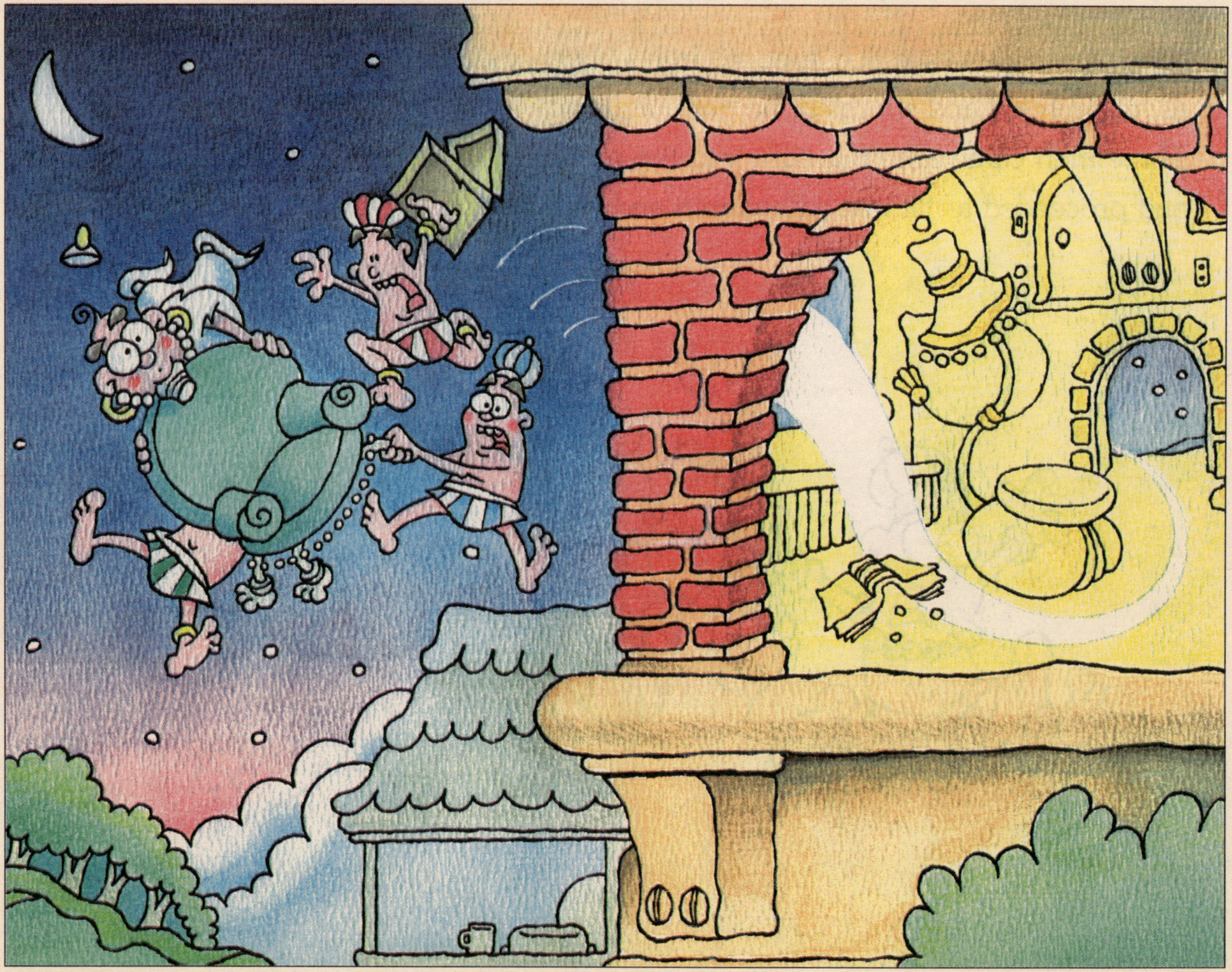

"Remember those hundreds of camels and sheep,
and the thousands of horses and donkeys you keep
in that field where you used to have millions of goats
by the lake where you always kept all of your boats,
and your barns and your pens and your coops and your stalls?
Well, some burglars came and they burgled it ALL!

But it doesn't end there 'cause those down-dirty stinkers
made off with your bangles and jingles and twinklers.
They snatched up your doodads and gizmos and blinkers!"

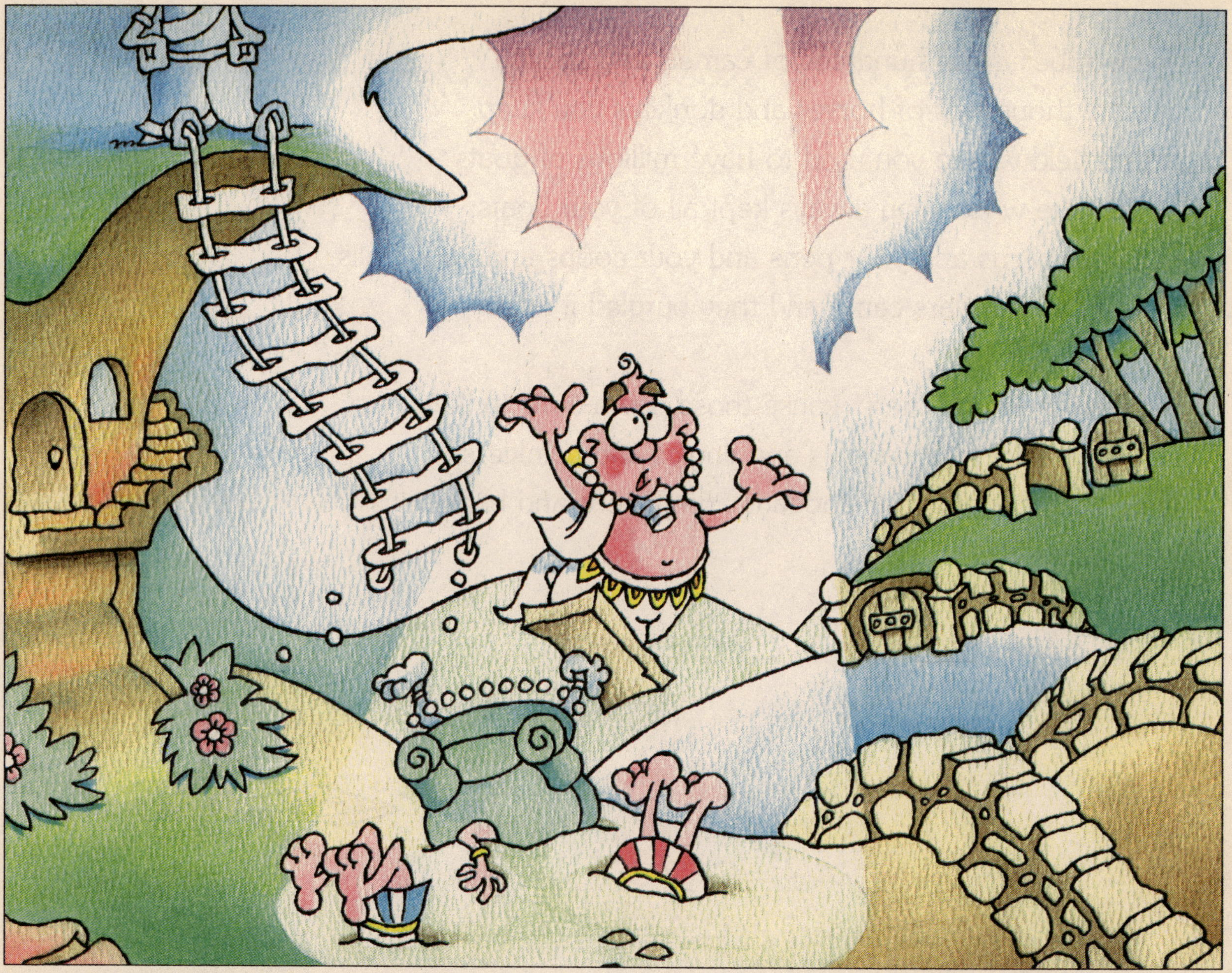

Poor Job was astounded. Completely dumbfounded!
His stomach glub-gurgled. His heart pumped and pounded.
But oh, don't you know, he got down on his knees.

He gave thanks to the Lord just as quick as you please!

"I just hate all that praising. It makes me quite ill!"
spat the devil. "But I can go one better still....
I'll give him some uh-ohs and boo-boos and stings!
Then I'll bet it's a whole different song that he sings!"

48

So Job became terribly, scare-ably sick.
He wheezled and woozled. He hacked and up-hicked!
"What good is your faith? It's a joke. It's a lie!
Give up!" Job's wife sputtered. "Just CURSE GOD AND DIE!"

"Curse God and die? Curse God and die!?
I cannot. I will not! But, why, oh Lord, WHY?"

News travels fast. Oh my yes, that's the truth!
And THIS news traveled straight to three friends from Job's youth
who took off right that minute, posthaste, P.D.Q.
to find out what was up, and see what they could do.

"It just isn't fair. No, it doesn't make sense.
This tragic, traumatical turn of events!
Lord, why be created, composed, or contrived
when I'm better not born, brought about, or alived!"

"Oh, give me a break!" Eliphaz blurted out.
"You've sinned a great sin. There can't be any doubt.
Just look at yourself. You're a mess! You're a wreck!
You've been up to no good, I suppose and suspect."

"Oh yes, we agree and as logic would show,
true enlightenment, knowledge, and learning, you know,
would have kept you from making that stupid mistake
of the kind and the type that we've known you to make."

"We KNOW that Job's utterly wicked and rotten,
but what does GOD think? That's the thing we've forgotten!
This punishment's awful. An outrage! A curse!
But it could have, and probably SHOULD have been worse!"

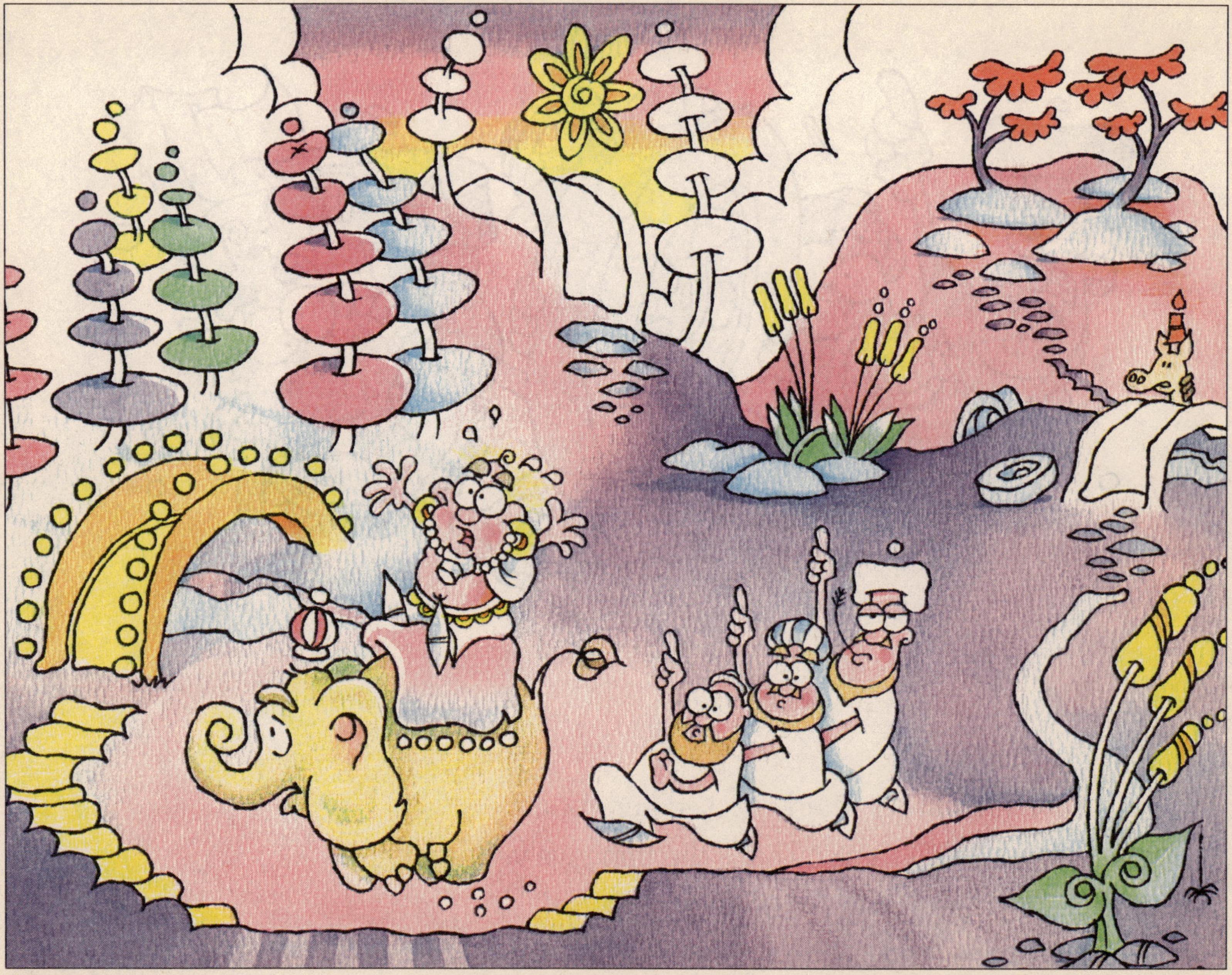

"What wonderful friends. What exquisite advice!
Did you say you were leaving? Yes, that would be nice!

I know that I'm righteous. I haven't a doubt.
My spirit is clean both within and throughout.
And although God destroys me and grinds me to dust,
it is Him whom I'll honor, abide in, and trust!

I've done nothing wrong. Yes, I KNOW that it's true.
So, tell me, Lord, **WHAT IN THE WORLD DID I DO?**"

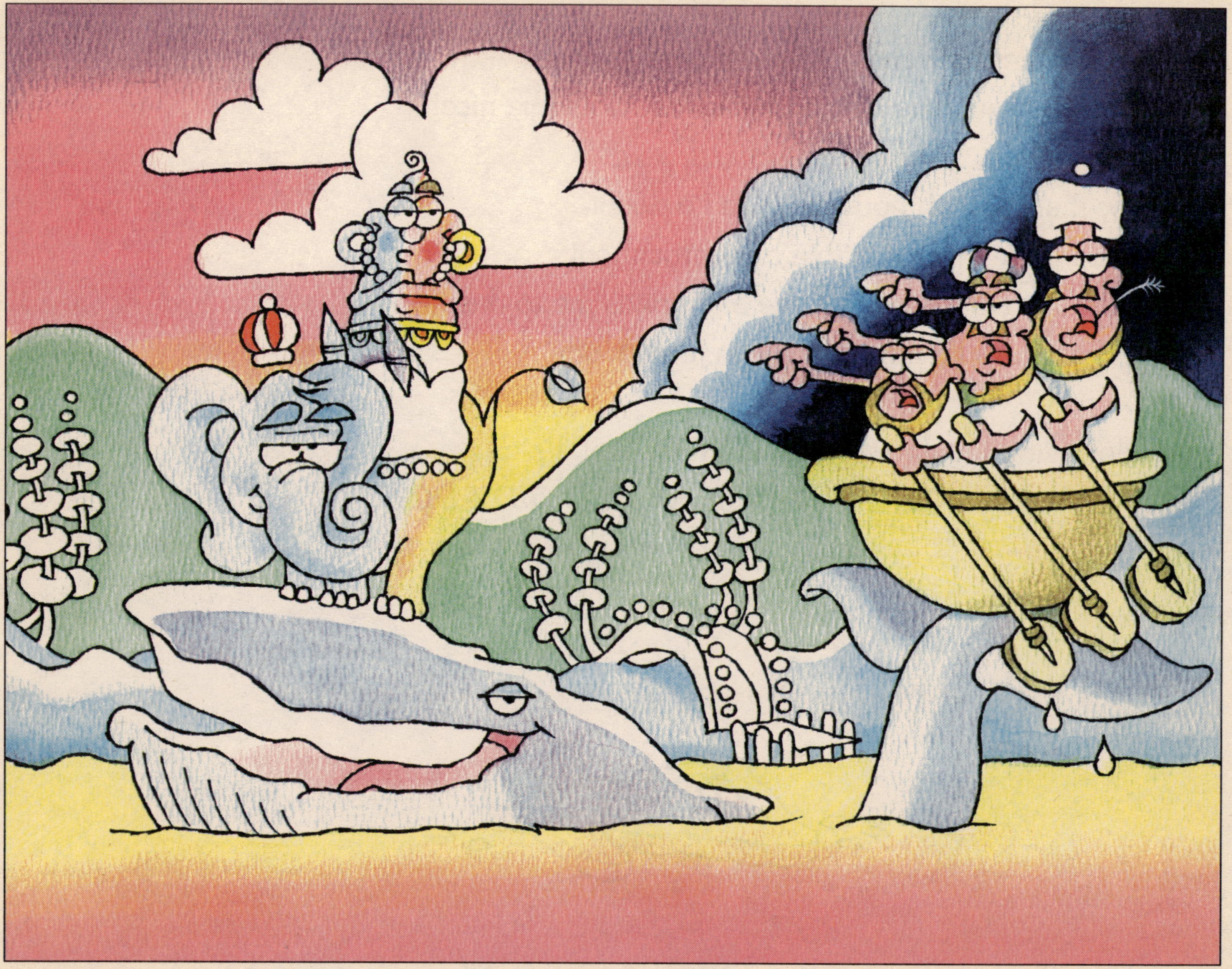

"What did you do? Oh, if we only knew!"

"You must have been lying or cheating or stealing.
Yes, snitching and sneaking and squawking and squealing.
Oh, how could you do it? Oh, what did you do?
Oh, why are we standing here talking to you?!"

"Just who do you think that you're duping and fooling?
We're full of it, Job! Full of wisdom and schooling.
Go on," Bildad babbled, "rave, rant, roar, and hiss,
but remember, YOU got your own self into THIS!"

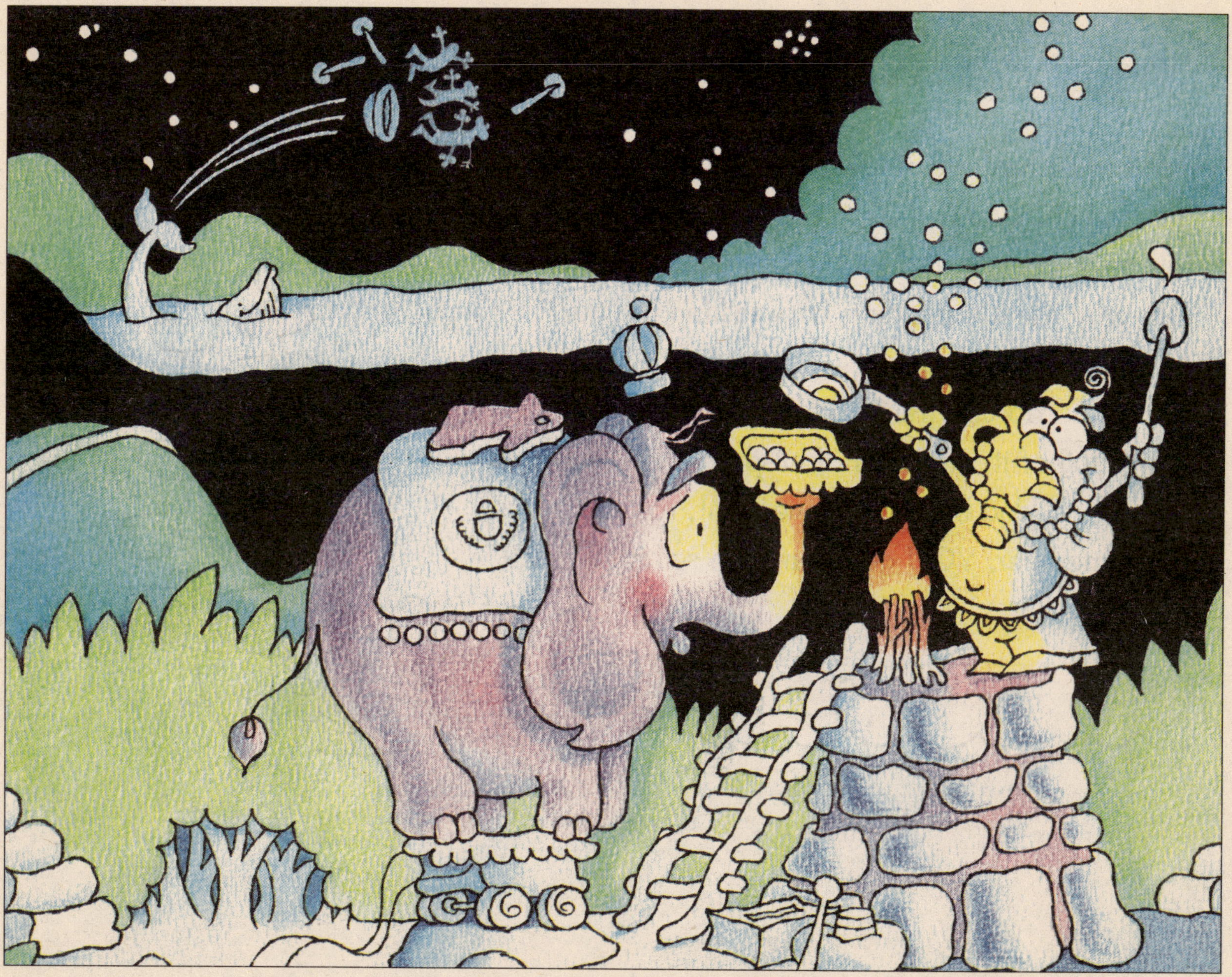

"Lord, why do You slay me? What gives You the right?
Has it done any good? Can it be Your delight?

You know that I'm righteous! I'm gentle and kind,
and our hearts are so sweetly, completely entwined.
Oh, why don't You answer? Oh, where is the man
who would bring us together? Send HIM, if You can!"

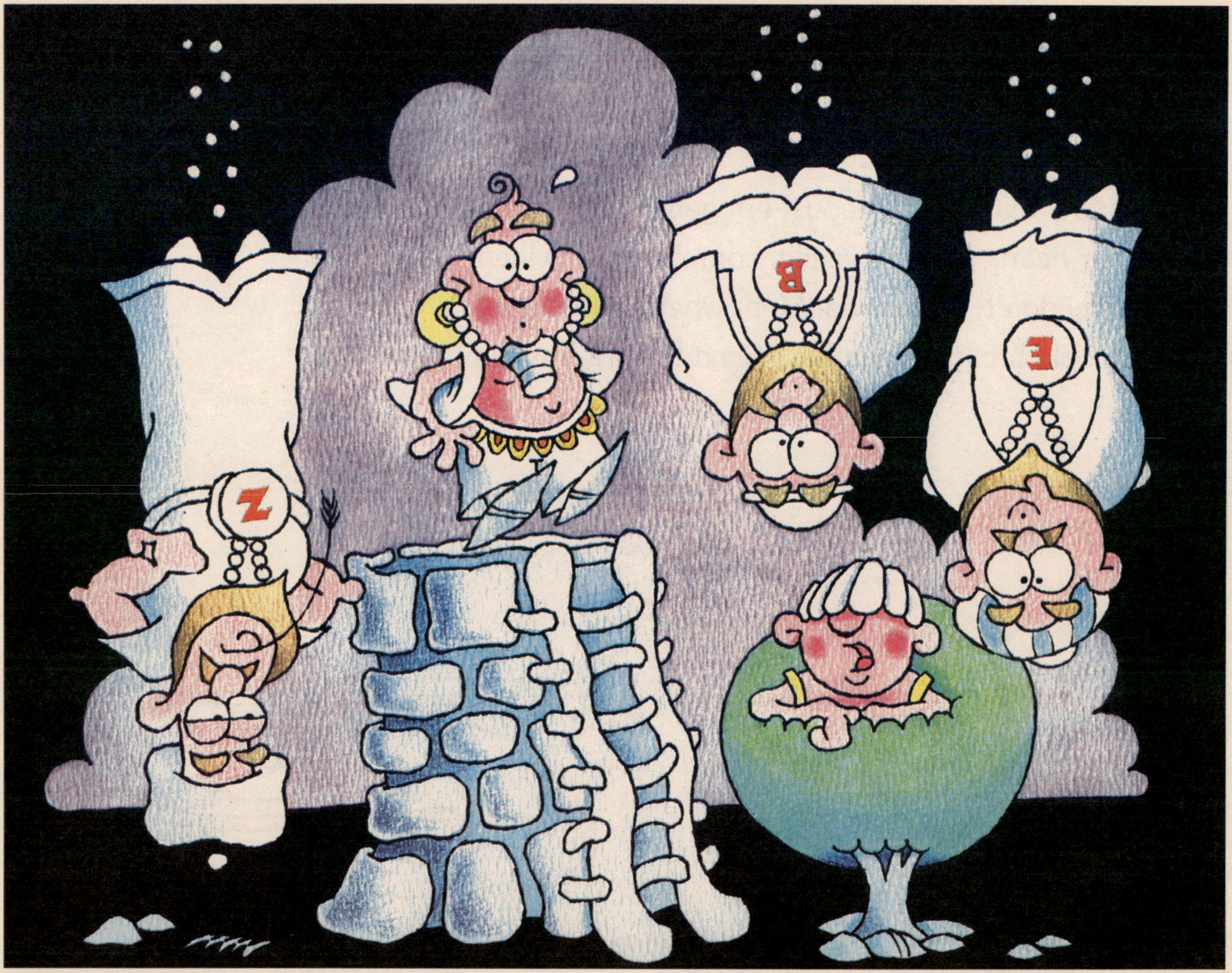

"Excuse me," said someone from back in the trees.
"Allow me to add my two cents, if you please:

These things I've been hearing!
These things you've been speaking!
This nonstop, right up to the eyeballs critiquing.
You speak against God. Boy, you've all got some guts!
What are you guys, crazy? What are you guys, nuts!?"

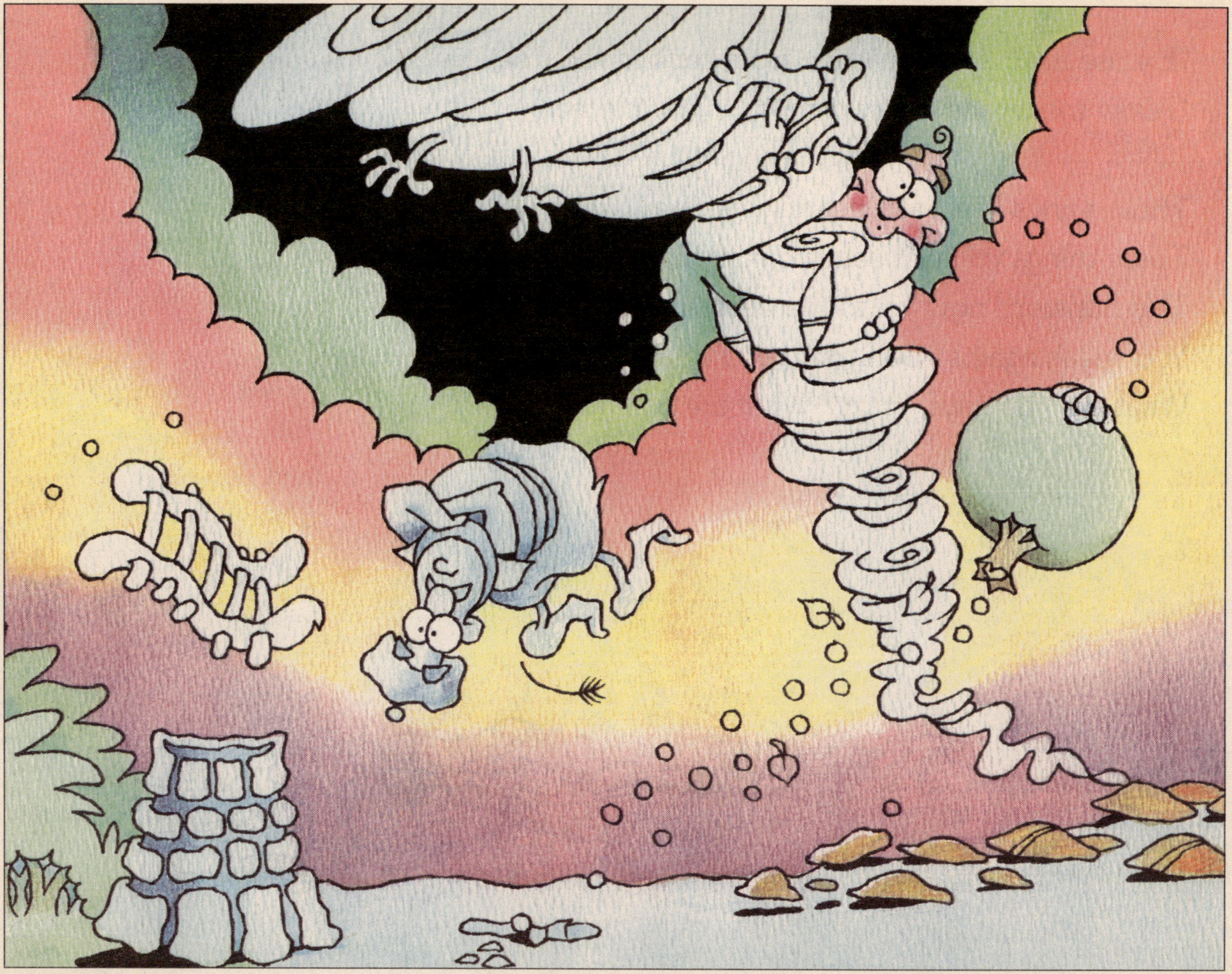

Well, those words weren't out of his mouth for one minute when the next thing I knew, we were standing there in it. Inside of a swirling, twist-twirling black cloud.
Then we all heard GOD'S voice. Very clear. VERY loud!

64

"Who filled up the oceans? Who turned on the stars?
Who brought forth Orion? The Milky Way? Mars?
Who made everything do the thing that it does?
Well I'll tell you: I did and I AM and I was!"

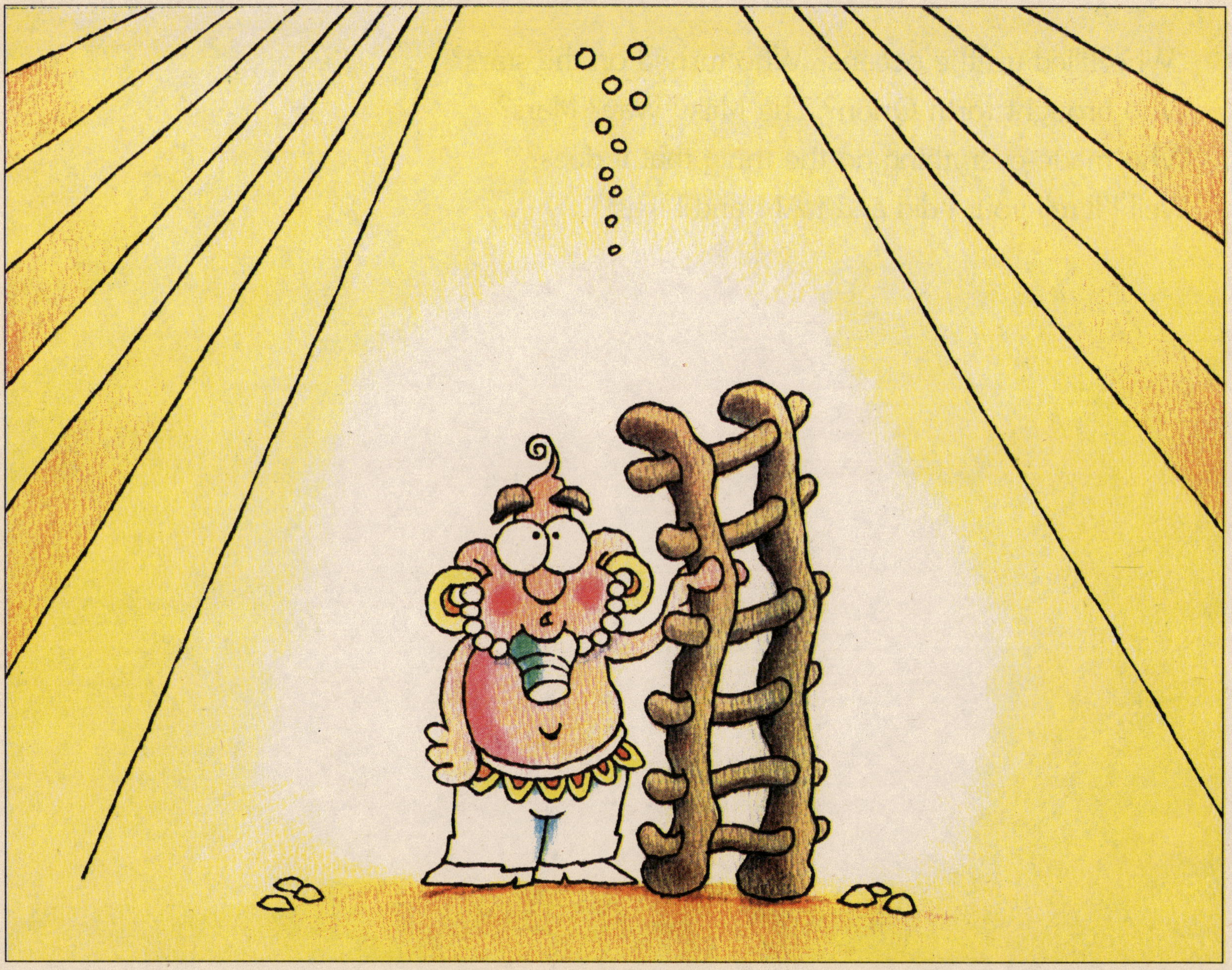

"Your home is with ME, Job. It isn't down here.

When all this is gone, all the why's and the how's,
all the to's and the fro's, all the here's and the now's,
there still will be you, and there still will be Me.
Together. Forever. Be patient. You'll see!"

Well, the Lord restored all of Job's cattle and goats,
his wife and his family, his friends and his boats.
And he lived to be more than one hundred and ten.
Very old. A bit wrinkled. Quite happy. Amen!

68

A JONAH DAY

The Story of Jonah

BY PHIL A. SMOUSE

A Barbour Book

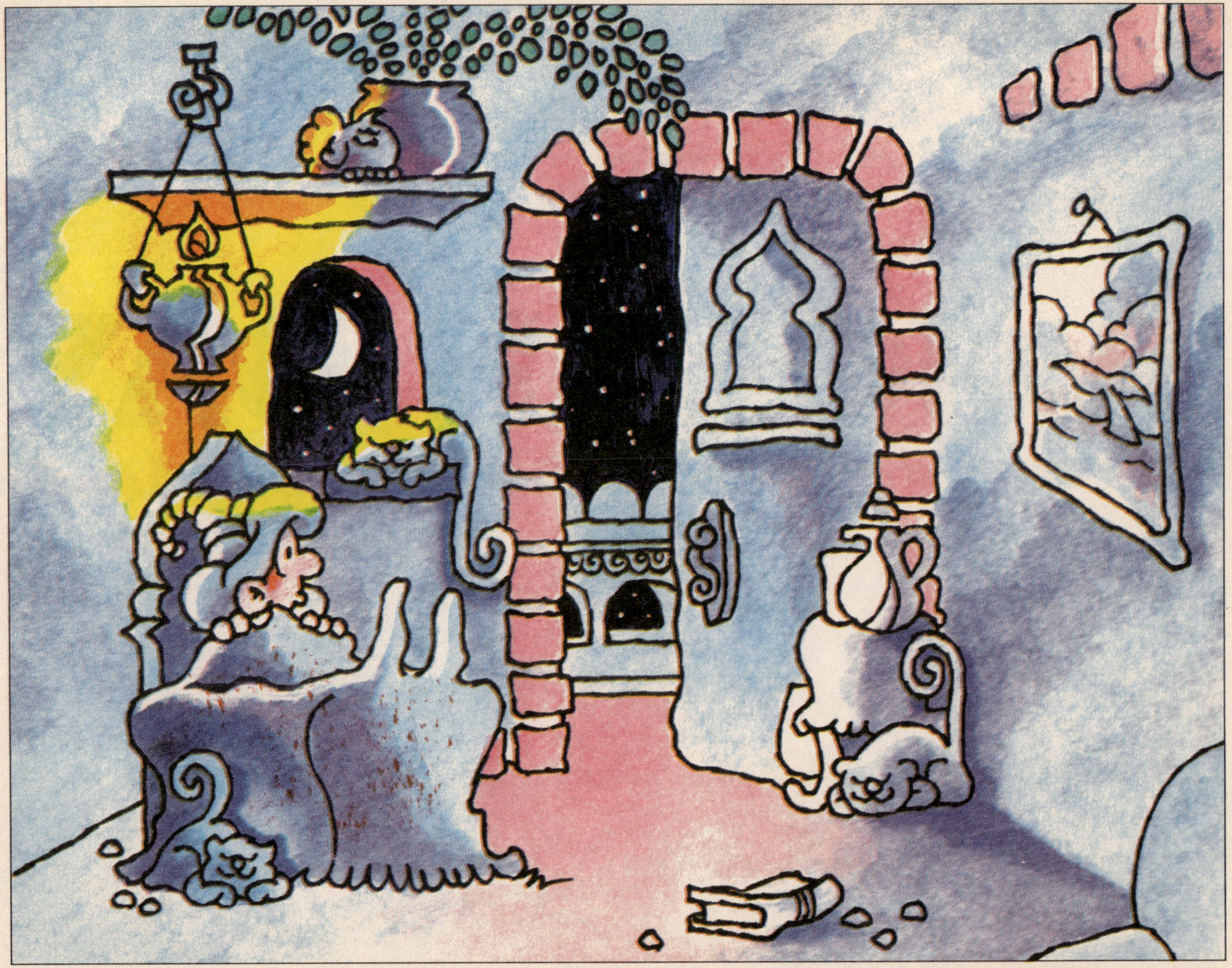

The Lord's word to Jonah came quite unexpected:
"Go down to Nineveh. You've been elected.
Tell all the people there, without delay,
this thing that I tell you to tell them today."

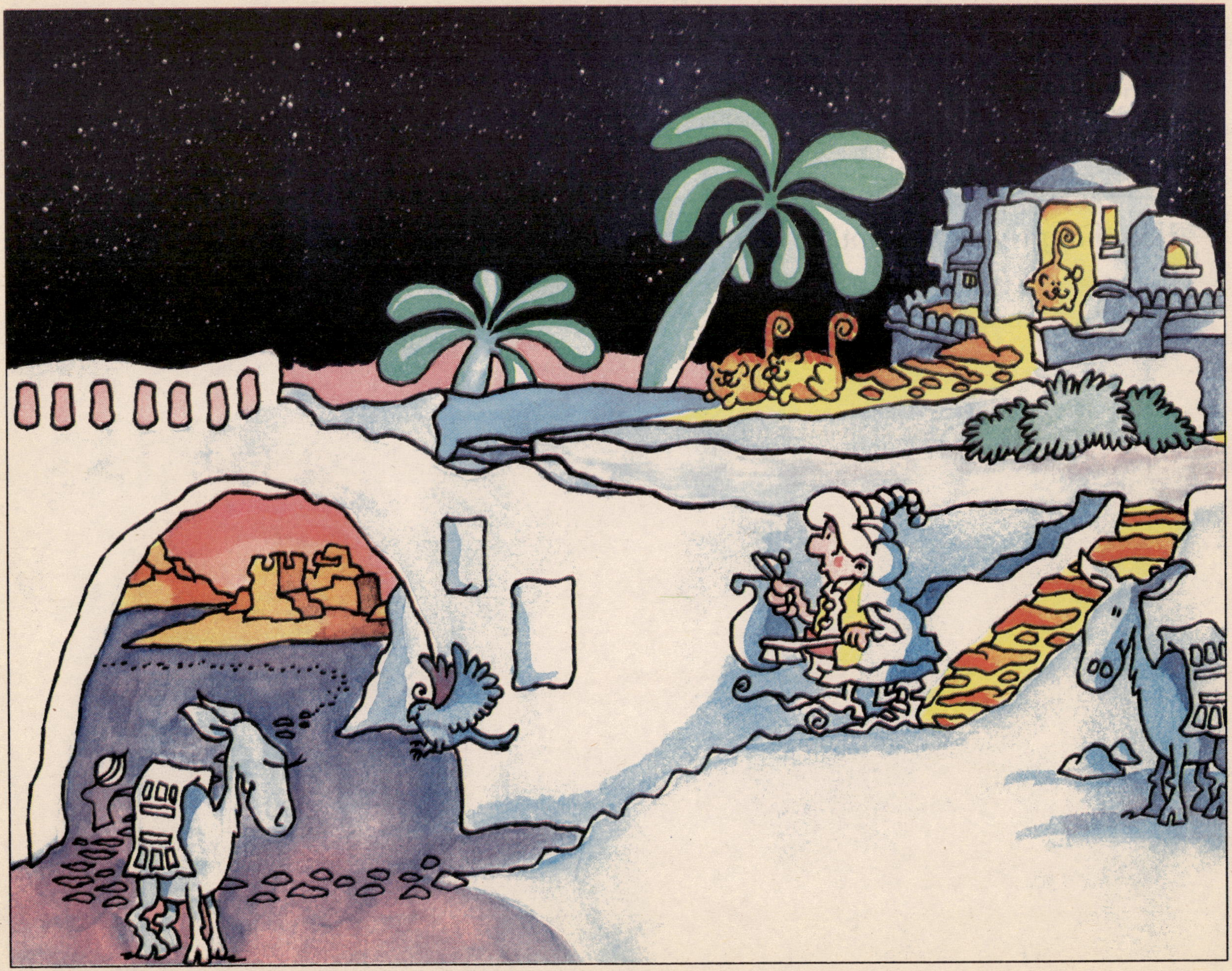

"Nineveh! Goodness! Of all of the places!
Those Ninevites all have the *nastiest* faces.
They're rude and they're crude and I'd have to conclude
they're an ill-tempered brood of the *worst* magnitude.

But I guess that I'll do it.
It *is* on my way.
Now *what* is it, Lord, that You want me to say?"

"THUS SAYS THE LORD! This is what you should say:
'Listen up, or I may have to ruin your day!

*You're all mean, and you're nasty, and not very nice,
and those are your GOOD points, to be more precise.
For I mean what I say, and I am quite sincere
when I tell you I smell you the whole way up here!'"*

"Tell *that* to *them?* You must be mistaken!
You certainly can't expect *me* to partake in
a dreadful, impossible scheme," Jonah spat,
"like the one You're suggesting and that, Lord, is *that!*"

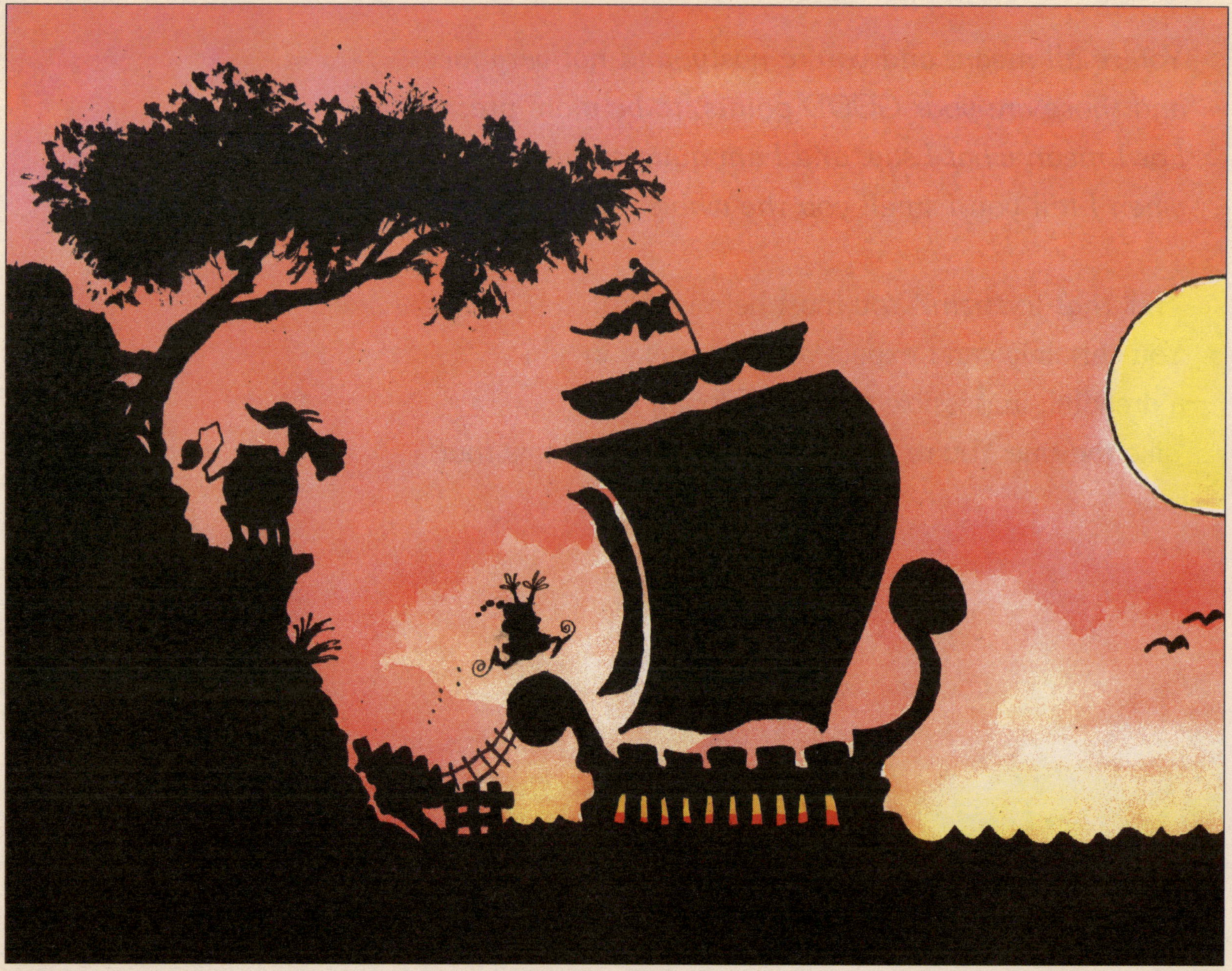

"How awful, how shocking, how horribly harsh-ish!"
he thought as he boarded a boat bound for Tarshish.
And down in the very most bottomest part
Jonah laid there alone, just himself and his heart.

Jonah laid in that boat, and he thought and he thought;
but he just *couldn't* do what he knew that he ought.
Now, you can't run away from the Lord, Jonah knew it.
But he was about to find out what occurs when you DO it!

The weather started getting rough. The tiny ship was tossed....

A tempest blew. The boat's crew flew!
The thunder boomed. "We're surely doomed!"
they all presumed, "to be consumed here by this holocaust!"

"All hands on deck,
all hands on deck!"
the captain shouted out.
"And Jonah, *you* get up here too!
Because, if I am not mistaken,
this earthquaking is the making
of the likes of you."

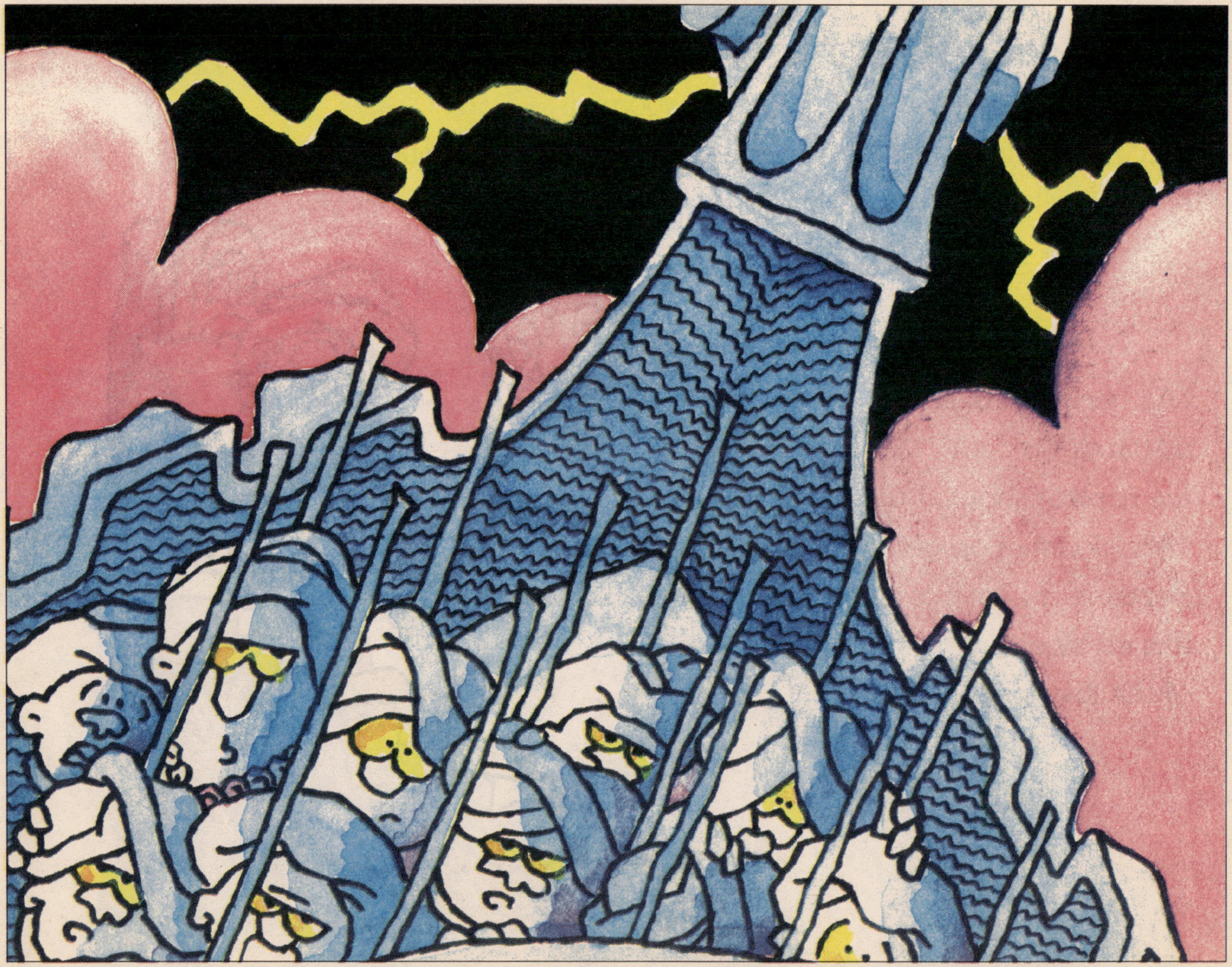

The crew drew straws to figure out just who should be ejected for causing this calamity to which they'd been subjected.

The shortest straw would tell them who, and as he had predicted, the captain watched with no surprise as good old Jonah picked it!

"Okay, okay, it's all my fault. Just throw me out. The storm will stop!"

"You heard the man. Let's throw him in!"
the sailors shouted with a grin.
"Yes, bon voyage and tally-ho,
let's pick him up and heave him, HO!"

"Wait a minute. Not so fast,"
the captain shouted, flabbergasted.
"Let's try again.
Let's make the shore.
Now grab your oars
and row some more.
*Stroke, stroke,
stroke, stroke!*"

But they simply couldn't do it....

So they threw him out in-TO it!

And, all at once, the thunder stopped.
The sea grew calm. The sun came out.
What God did Jonah so betray
to cause this startling display
where even wind and waves obey?

(Now deeper and deeper he found himself sinking,
which prompted old Jonah to do some rethinking!)

"Oh Lord," Jonah cried, "have You left me for dead?
The waves and the waters encircle my head.
Barnacles clutch at my fingers and toes,
and some wet, wiggly thing is attached to my nose!

Oh, there's nothing, I'm sure, quite so dreadful as this…

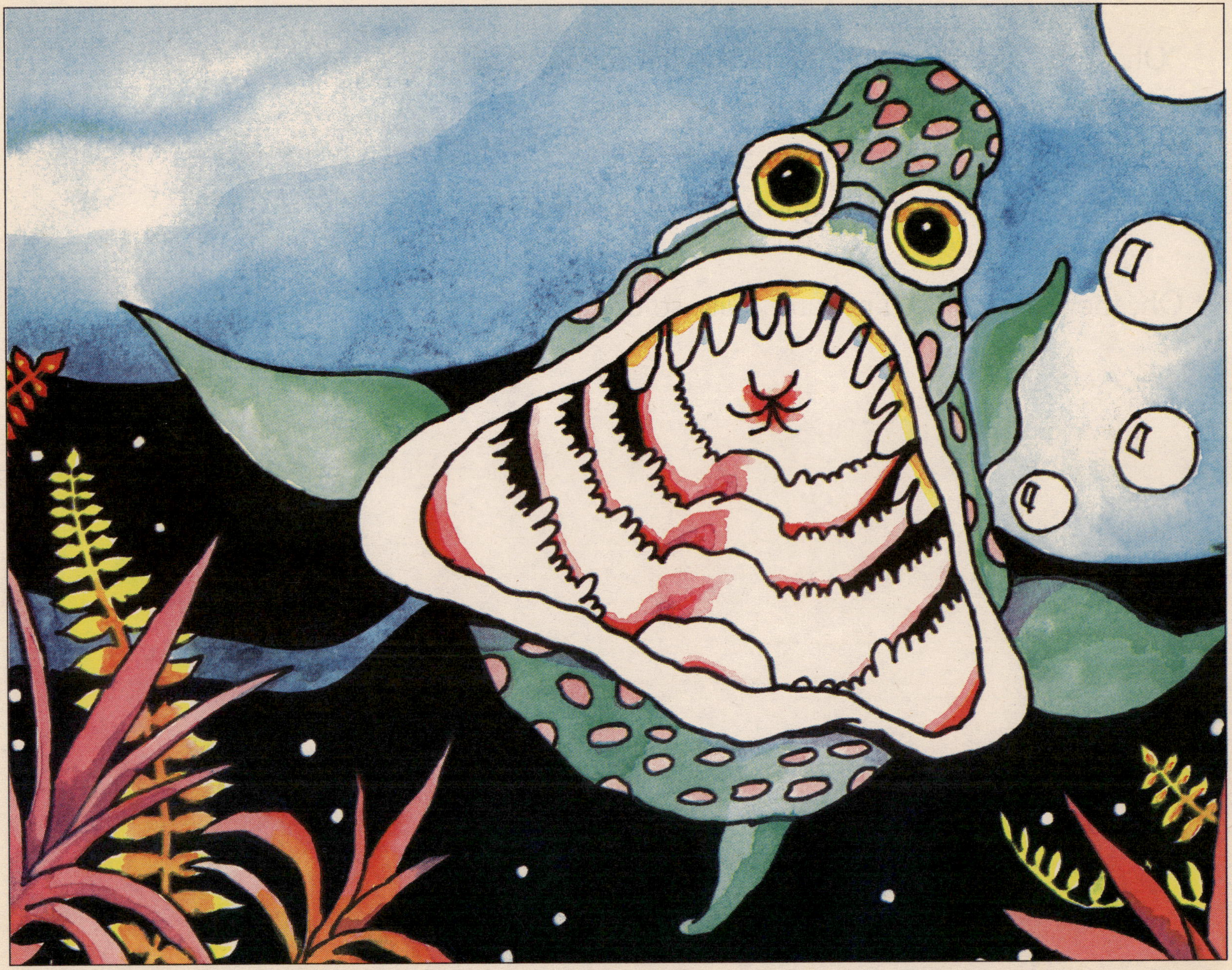

except being swallowed alive by a fish!"

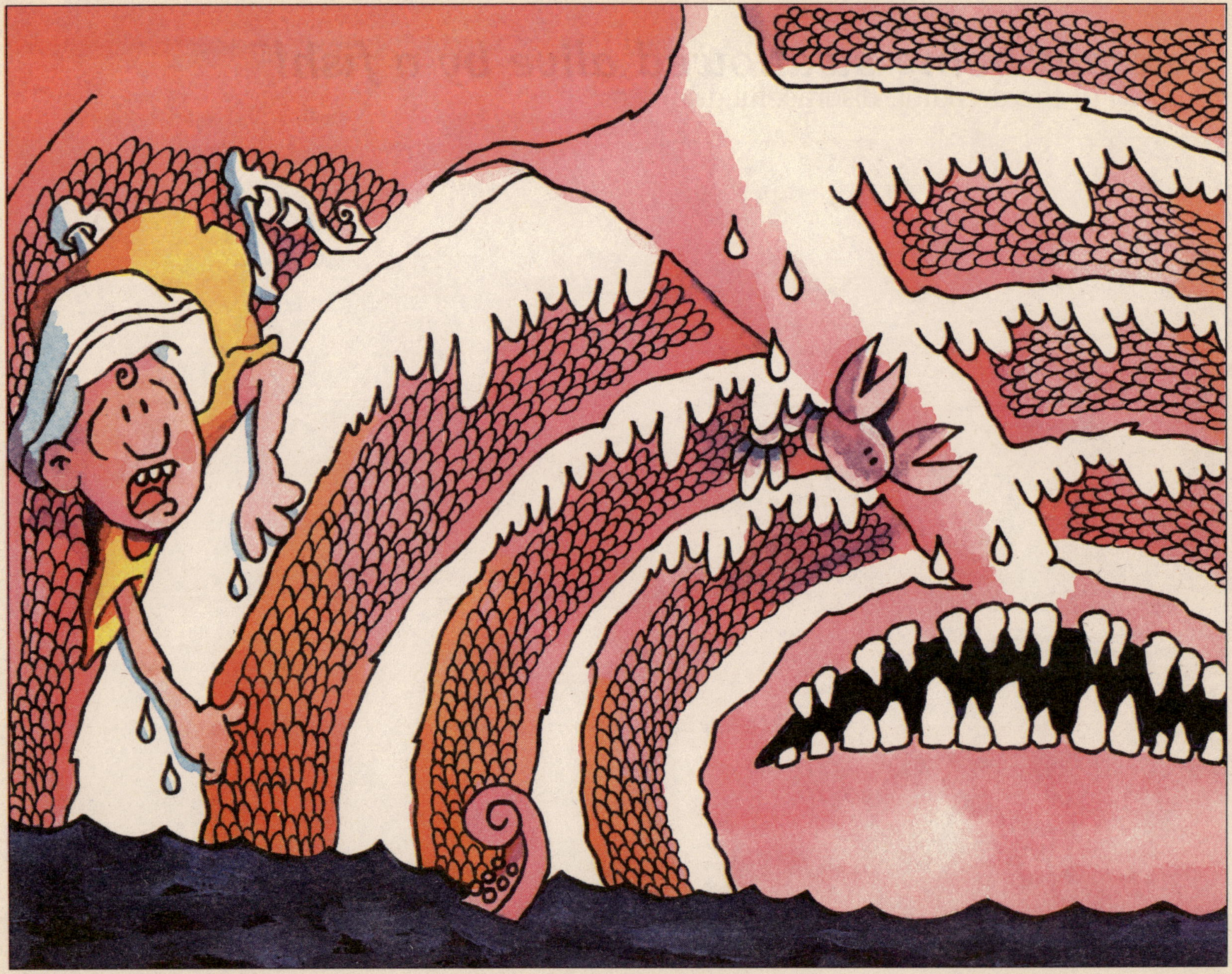

"Inside of a fish! Oh, of all of the places!
Of all of the dreadful, disgraceful disgraces!
I'll do what You ask, Lord! I'll do it Your way.
I'll do it right now, right this minute, *today*."

So that fish spat up Jonah right there on the beach;
and the minute it did, Jonah started to preach.

"'**Forty more days,** says the Lord. It's a fact.
You've got forty short days left to clean up your act.

For you're mean, and you're nasty and not very nice;
And those are your good points, to be more precise.
Yes, I mean what I say and I am quite sincere
when I tell you I smell you the whole way up here.'

IS THAT CLEAR?"

94

Now, everyone there from the king straight on down
was convinced that this guy wasn't fooling around.
So they cleaned up their hearts.
Yes, they cleaned up their act.
And they cleaned it up quick, as a matter of fact.

But forty days passed, and then forty-one,
and the Lord didn't do what He said would be done.

"Lord, what's
going on there?
I look like a goof.

You said You'd
destroy them.
Now give me
some proof!"

"Proof, my friend Jonah?
You don't understand.
All of creation
is at My command!

And no matter how angry
or hurtful or mean,
unfaithful, unworthy,
or selfish you've been,
I'll never reject you
or turn you away.
(For I love you so deeply,
I barely can say.)

I'm waiting,
just WAITING
to open My hands...."

"And that's why I gave them, and YOU,
one more chance."

PETE, FEET, AND FISH TO EAT

The Story of Peter

BY PHIL A. SMOUSE

A Barbour Book

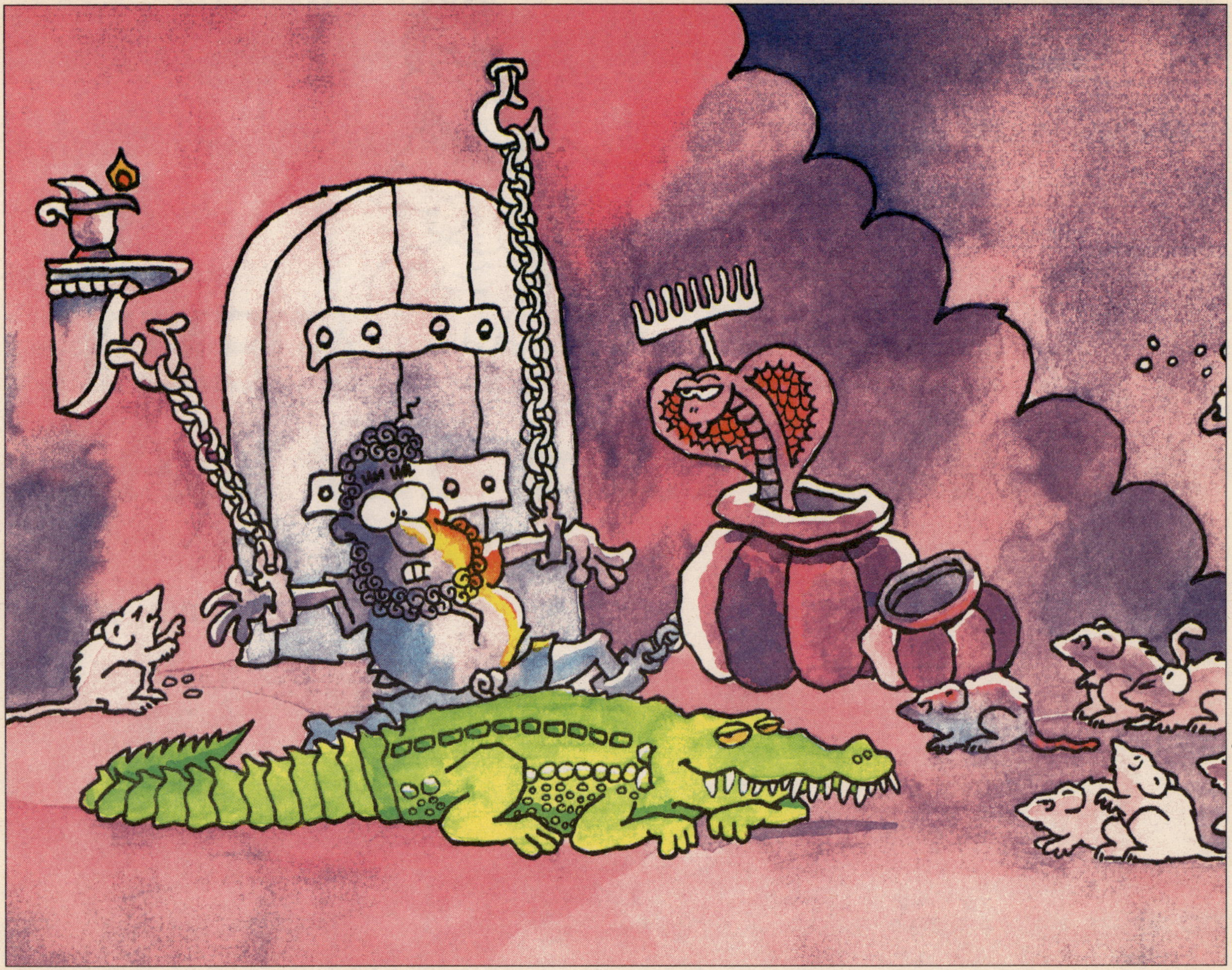

Fantastic! Amazing! They'll never believe it.
It's such a surprise, I can hardly conceive it.

An hour ago, I was locked in a cell
full of jeeper creep-peepers and dust-musty smells.
I was chained to the wall. I was chained to the door.
I was chained to the lamp and the chair and the floor!

Then a voice, still and small, like a beautiful light,
whispered, "Peter, look up!" and to my great delight...

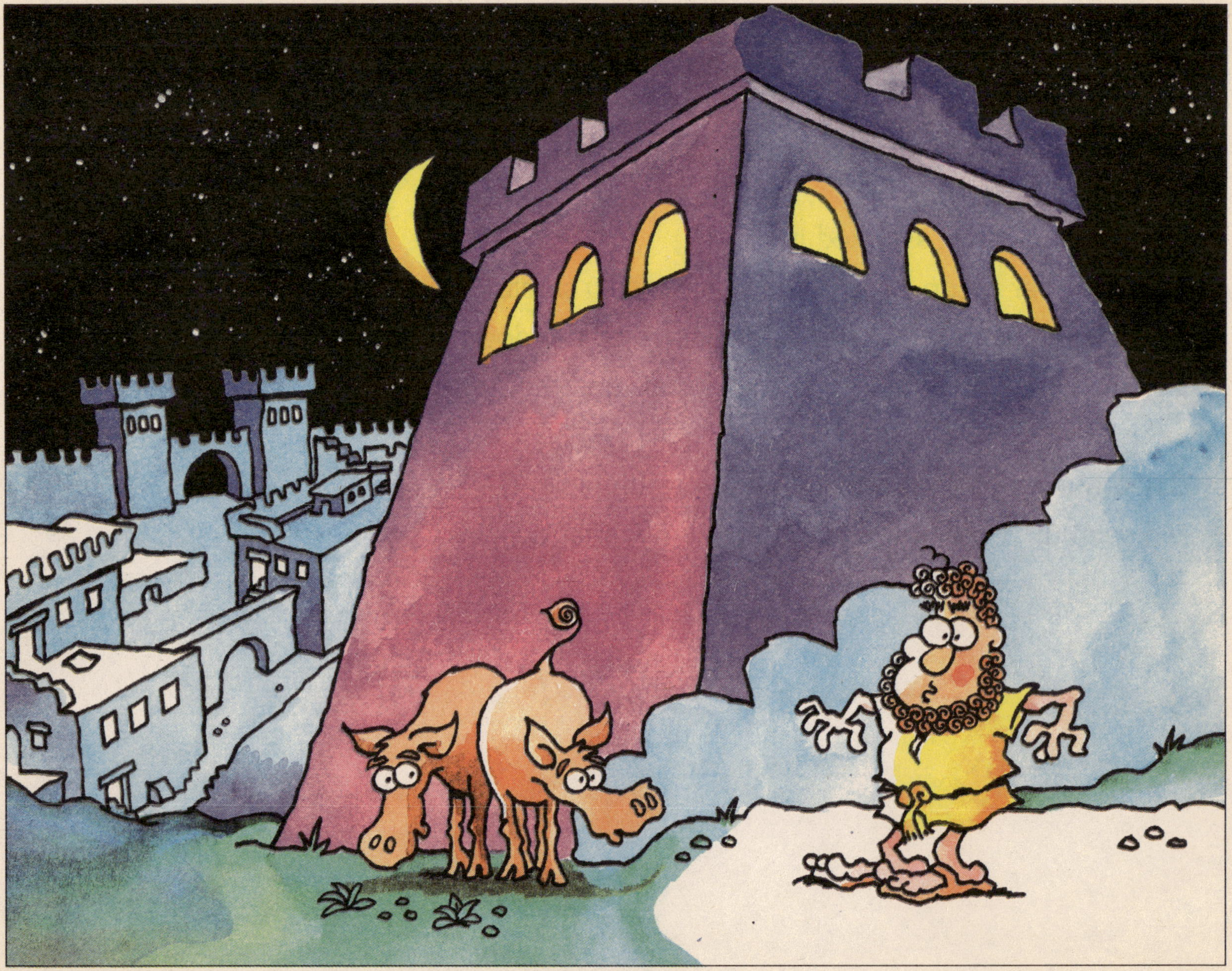

My chains were all broken. I was up on my feet.
I was out of that prison and back on the street!

Now, as you might have guessed, I was rather excited
to be so completely removed and uprighted.
I flew down the alley. I kicked up the dust.
I raced through the darkness, full speed ahead plus...

Finish the story? Get on with it? Do it?!
All right, just sit tight, and I'll get around *TO* it!

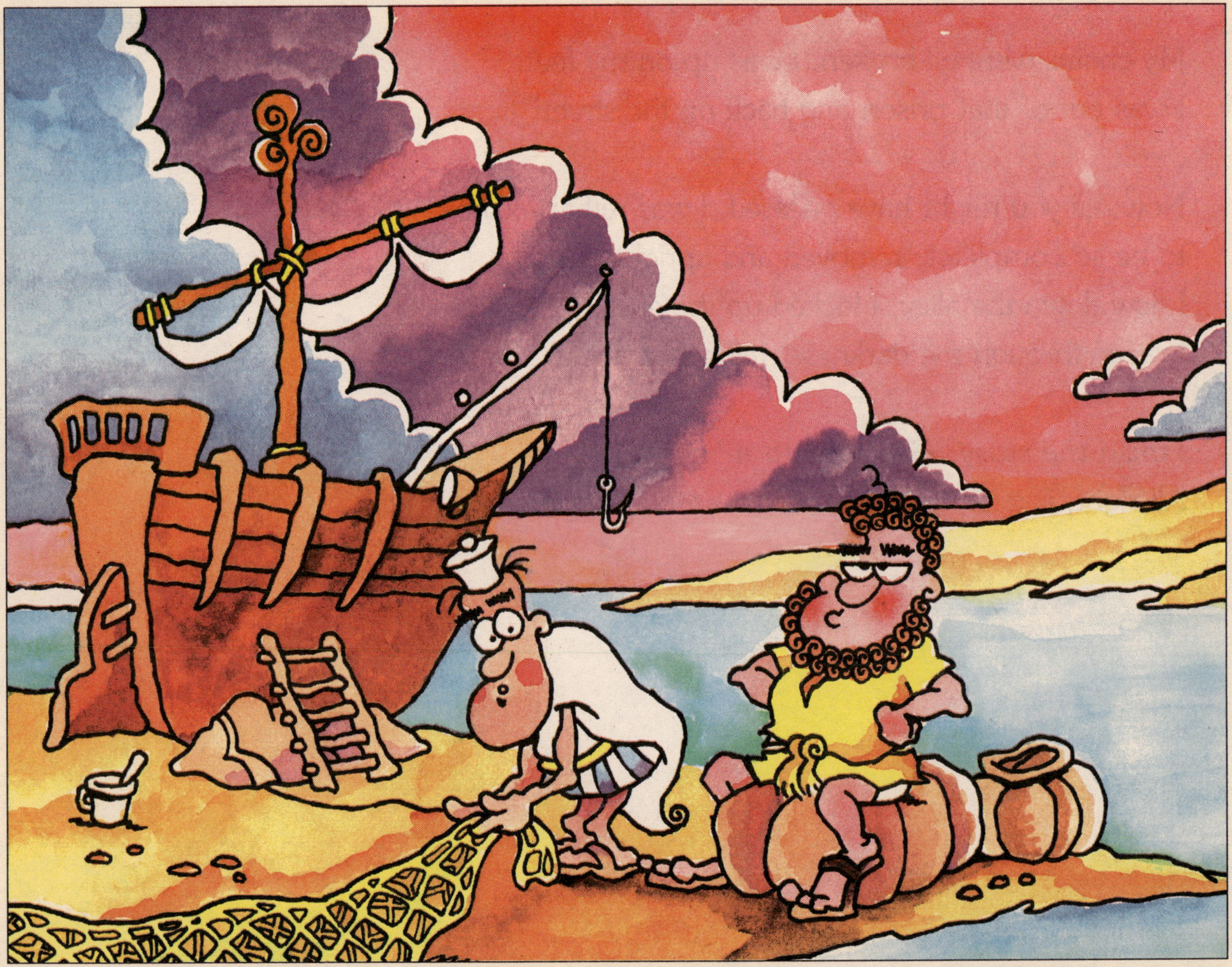

"Start at the start." That's what Mom used to say.
There was just no forgetting that one certain day...
We were washing our nets. We'd been fishing all night,
and my brother and I had a terrible fight.

"It's a beautiful fish, I would tend to agree,
and the only one singular fish that I see!
After thirty-one hours of huffing and sweating,
there's one teeny, tiny, small thing you're forgetting.

One trivial, trifling, petty, slim thought:

IN A DAY AND A HALF,
THIS IS ALL THAT
WE'VE CAUGHT!"

I was frothing and foaming, steaming and stewing, yes, gritting and grinding and chafing and chewing!

I was so caught away in my little black cloud that I never did notice the wonderful crowd of a hundred, or maybe a thousand or more, who squash-squeezed and crunch-crowded their way to the shore.

"Teach us, O Lord!" I heard them all shout
as they hustled and bustled and rustled about.

And there went my brother. He was shouting it, too.
Why, the place had turned into
some kind of a zoo!

Well, *that's* when it happened.
He came up to *me*,
this man they were eyeing
and trying to see.

He stepped into my boat, and He asked for a lift;
so I hoisted the sail, and I set her adrift.

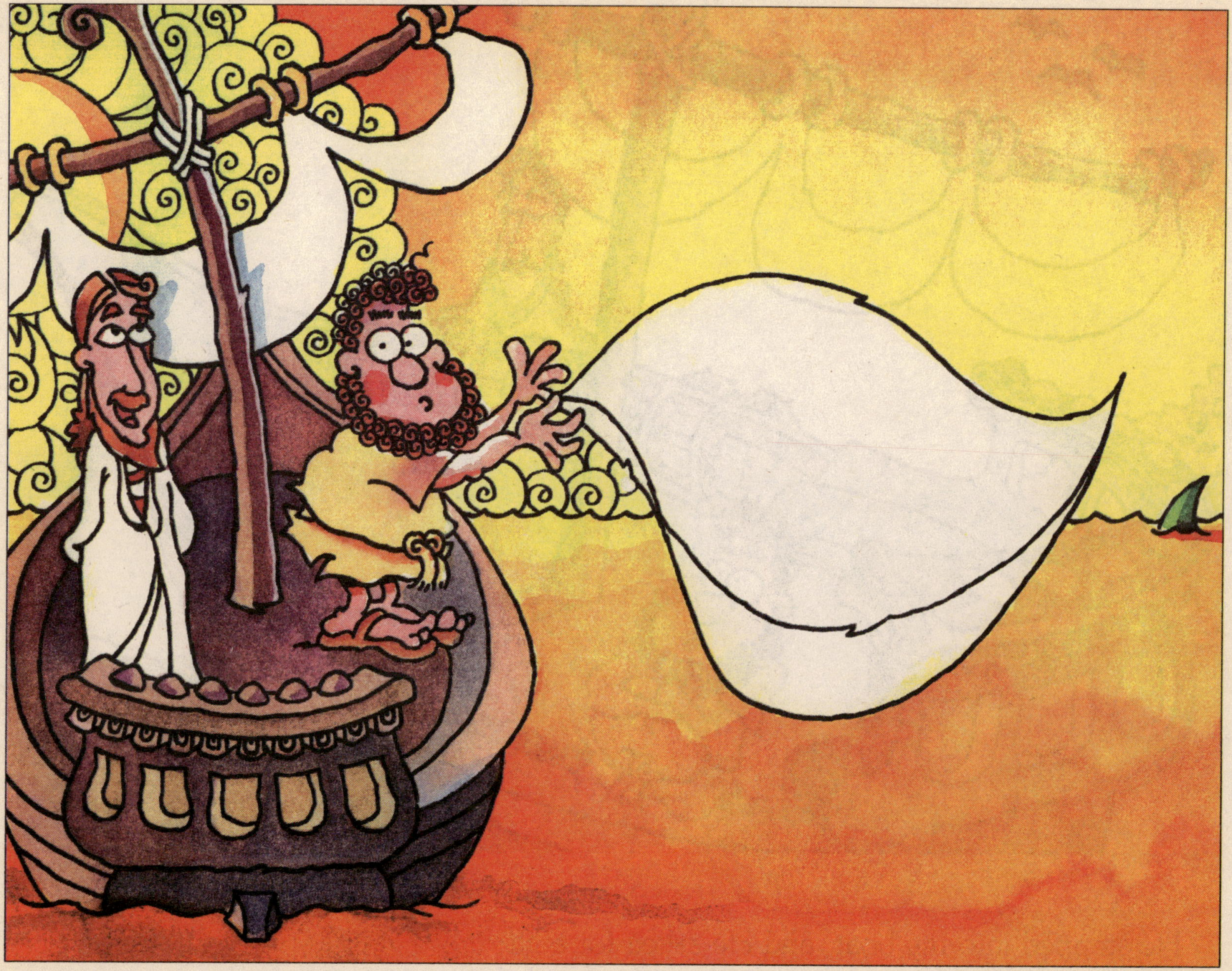

"Cast out your nets," He proclaimed, "if you wish,
and you'll find that they're filled full to bursting with fish."

"Whatever you say...." (This should really be good!)
We'll probably snag a few pieces of wood,
or maybe some cans or a shoe or a boot
or a water-logged wallet. Now *that* would be cute!

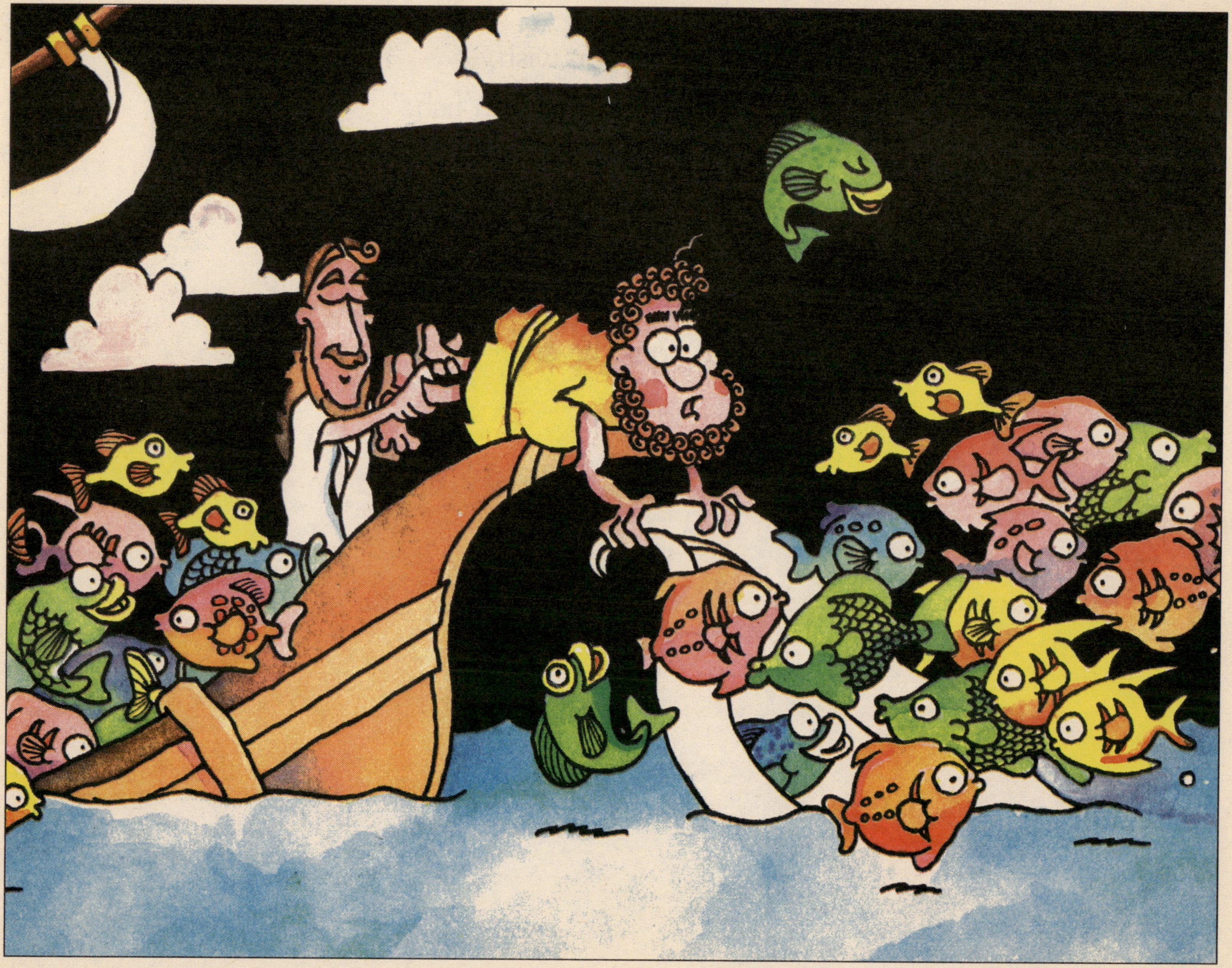

What happened next was a little bit shocking.
It sent my head spinning. It set my knees knocking!

Fish by the tens and the hundreds of dozens—
fish uncles and aunts, nephews, nieces, and cousins—
were cramming my nets. And before I could blink,
my poor boat was so full that it started to sink.

"Oh, Lord!" I cried out as I fell at His feet
and proceeded to whimper and sniffle and bleat.

"Go away from me. Please, please, just leave me alone!
I'm the worst kind of horrible man ever known."

But HE didn't care. It was perfectly fine.
I could tell as His eyes looked down deep into mine.
And right then and there, in that boat, on that day,
Jesus wiped all my badness and sadness away.

(But if you think *that's* something, then listen to this,
because *this* will be something you won't want to miss....)

I remember that night us guys were recollecting

as we laughed and we hugged, all the while interjecting.

But amid the munching and crunching and chewing,

I noticed this strange thing that Jesus was doing.

He'd taken a bowl and a towel and a seat, and proceeded to wash every one of our feet. Our *feet,* of all things! Yes, He sat there among us. He plucked every toe-jam and flushed every fungus!

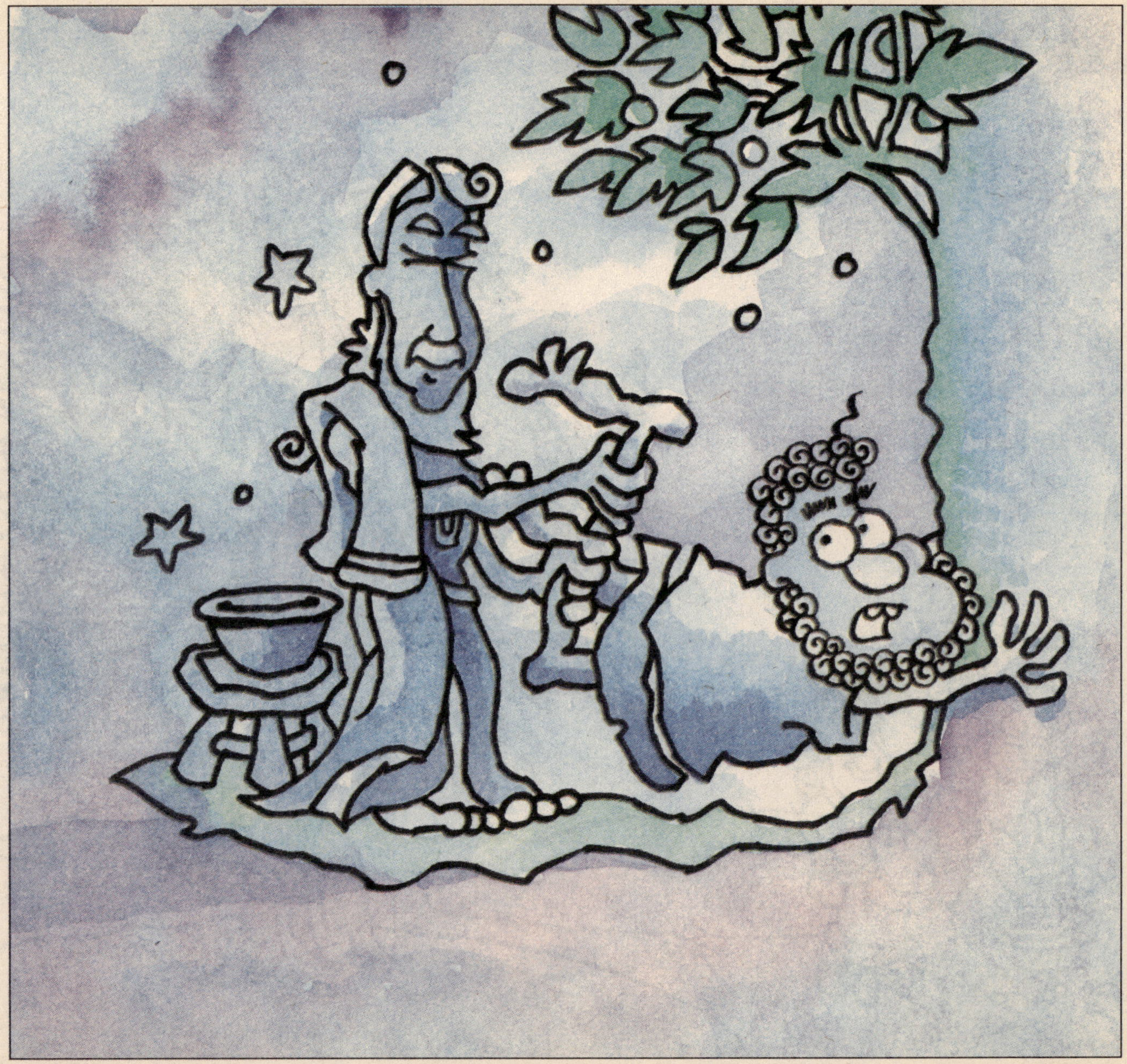

"Not *my* feet, Lord! No, they are not for You to clean!"
(Isn't there something *wrong* with this scene?)
"I'm certain there's something *important* to do
For someone who's someone like someone like You...."

Well, He looked at that bowl, and I knew in a minute
He wanted my two big, fat feet to be in it!

"All right, then," I blathered, "well, how about this...

I'll go get a sponge and a mop and a hose,
and we'll scrubble and bubble
    my knees and my nose.
Then we'll wish-wash my eyebrows
and swish-swash my hips.
We'll polish my forehead
and lather my lips!"

"Calm down. Pull the plug,
Peter. Put it on ice!
Can't you see that I'm trying
to do something nice?"

"Just relax," Jesus whispered, "and listen up well,
because now *I'm* the one with a story to tell!"

The story He told us was shocking and frightening.
Our eyes were bug-bulging, our stomachs twist-tightening.

He said He'd be battered, bruised, beaten and *killed*;
but the Word of the Lord would at last be fulfilled!
Then, to top it all off, He said I
would deny
that I ever did know
Him! "Oh, no, Lord!" I cried.

"Before the cock crows, you'll
deny Me three times."
How I wished I could
get those words out of my mind.

As they dragged Him away,
we were yelling and screaming.
This can't be for real.
I just have to be dreaming!

"Hey, you with the beard and the big bony knees,
come on over here, I'd like to talk to you, please!
I know your face, and I know it quite well.
You were with Him, that Jesus. I know. I can tell!"

"Mind your own business! Get out of my sight!
I don't know Him, OR YOU, so just drop it, all right?"

"We know you were there,
you could hardly be missed."
"You're mistaken!" I bellowed
and boiled and hissed.
"Yes, I saw him, too.
There can't be any doubt!"
an old, gravelly-gray,
dusty voice gurgled out.

"I DON'T KNOW THE MAN! Would you all just be QUIET! Please, leave me alone. Be still, calm down, come on now, let's try it!"

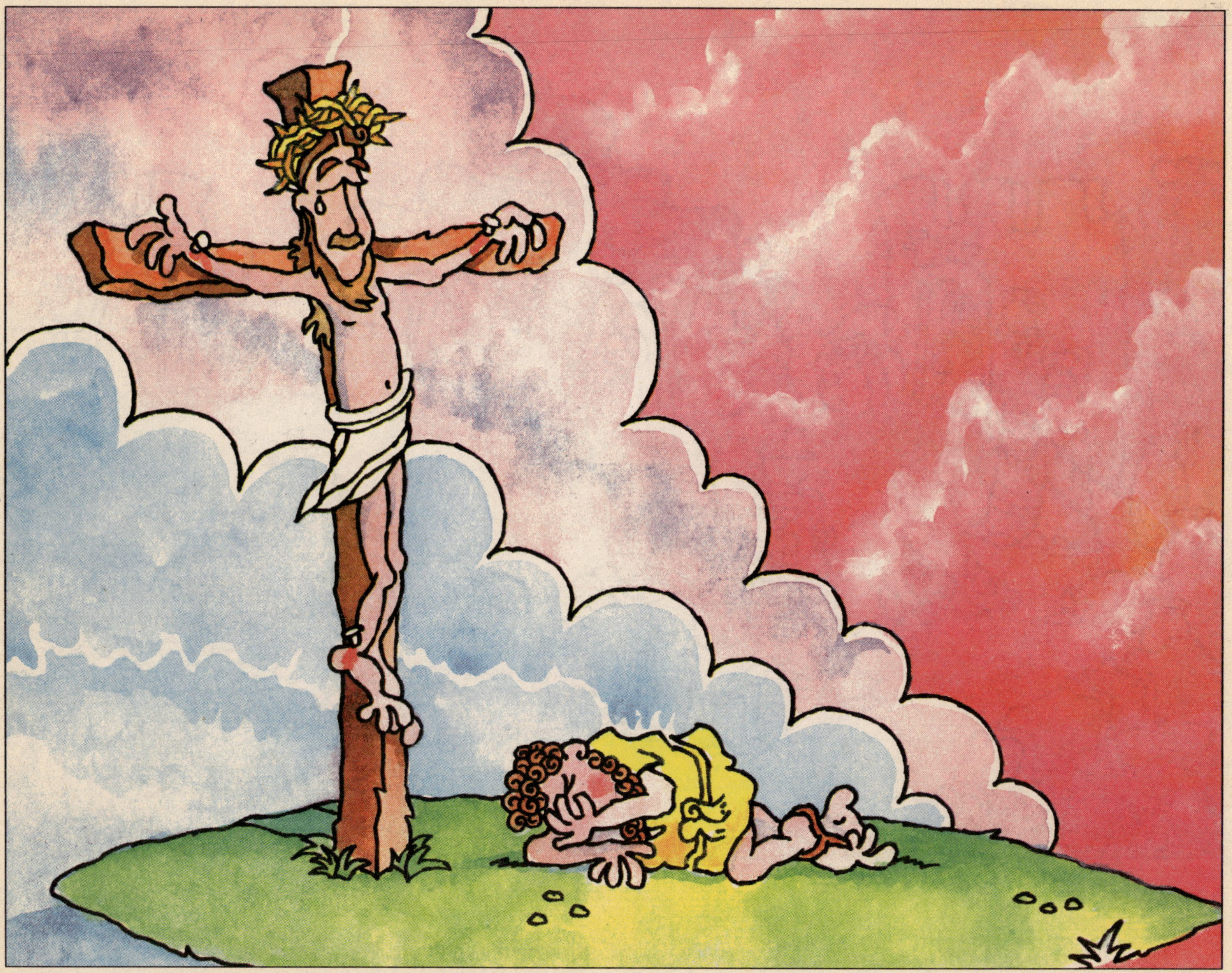

Yes, I denied Him, and they crucified Him.
I watched as they did it. I stood right beside Him.
But there's something I think that you really should know.
It's something He told me a long time ago...

"Peter," He said, "I AM LOVE, and you'll find
that I'm ever so patient and wonderfully kind.
I'm NOT keeping a list. I'm NOT checking it twice.
No, THAT would be naughty and not at all nice."

Oh, I've messed it up now. Lord, I've messed it up then.
Yes, I've messed it up over and over again.
Dear Lord Jesus, forgive me. Please bring me back home.
I'm the worst kind of horrible man ever known.

The past is forgotten. Erased! Oh, it's true.
He did it for me. He *WILL* do it for you!